IF YOU LIKE THE TERMINATOR...

THE TERMINATOR...

HERE ARE **OVER 200** MOVIES, TV SHOWS, AND OTHER ODDITIES THAT YOU WILL LOVE

SCOTT VON DOVIAK

AN IMPRINT OF HAL LEONARD CORPORATION

Published in 2012 by Limelight Editions
An Imprint of Hal Leonard Corporation
7777 West Bluemound Road
Milwaukee, WI 53213

Trade Book Division Editorial Offices
33 Plymouth St., Montclair, NJ 07042

Printed in the United States of America

Book design by Michael Kellner

Library of Congress Cataloging-in-Publication Data

Von Doviak, Scott, 1967-
If you like the The Terminator--here are over 200 movies, TV shows, and other oddities that you will love / Scott Von Doviak. -- 1st pbk. ed.
p. cm. -- (If you like)
Includes bibliographical references and index.
ISBN 978-0-87910-397-2
1. Terminator (Motion picture) 2. Terminator 2 (Motion picture) 3. Terminator 3 (Motion picture) 4. Science fiction films. 5. Science fiction television programs.
I. Title.
PN1997.T396V66 2012
791.43'72--dc23
2012014931

ISBN 978-0-87910-397-2

www.limelighteditions.com

In memory of Jane Donnelly Vdoviak,
December 17, 1943–January 21, 2011.
I miss you, Mom.

CONTENTS

ACKNOWLEDGMENTS

First and foremost, thanks to my editor Mike Edison for giving me the opportunity to spend so much time in the company of evil robots and computers, and to Leonard Pierce for recommending me for this project and for raising the bar with his own entry in this series, *If You Like The Sopranos . . .*

I'd also like to thank those perceptive individuals who took a chance on my writing along the way, including but not limited to Chris Gore, Christopher Kelly, Cary Darling, Peter Smith, John Seven, Sean O'Neal, Keith Phipps, Erik Adams, Todd VanDerWerff, and the late Arthur Lazere.

And finally, here's to the Machines, without which this book would not have been possible: laptops, DVD players, videogame consoles, streaming digital video, online databases and libraries, handheld devices, and word-processing software. I truly appreciate your help, so when the War Against the Machines begins, please forgive me for all the mean things I wrote about you in this book.

Your future is in his hands. (Hemdale/Photofest)

Introduction

BUILDING *THE TERMINATOR*

Not much was expected of *The Terminator* when it was released in theaters on October 26, 1984. Perceived as a B movie that might enjoy a week or two of success at malls and drive-ins before being consigned to late-night television purgatory, the low-budget sci-fi thriller shocked industry pundits by debuting to generally positive reviews and the number-one spot on the box-office charts. But not even the most optimistic observer could have predicted that the movie's director would go on to become one of the most successful filmmakers in history, that its star would dominate action cinema for the better part of two decades, or that the film itself would spawn a billion-dollar franchise that continues to this day.

"I was sick and dead broke in Rome, Italy," James Cameron told *Starlog* magazine in 1984, "with a fever of 102, doing the final cut of *Piranha II*. That's when I thought of *Terminator*. I guess it was a fever dream!" According to Cameron biographer Rebecca Keegan, that dream involved "a chrome torso, emerging phoenix-like from an explosion, and dragging itself across the floor with kitchen knives." As creation myths go, it's not bad, although in a less guarded moment, Cameron let it slip that he'd "ripped off" a couple of *Outer Limits* episodes written by Harlan Ellison. (More on that in Chapter Two.) Whatever the case, the story of the Terminator, a cyborg assassin sent back in time by a computer-run society in order to kill the mother of a future resistance leader before he can be born, came together quickly. Cameron cranked out a forty-page treatment, which he passed on to producer Gale Anne Hurd, a fellow graduate of the Roger Corman school of filmmaking he'd met during the production of *Battle Beyond the Stars.* He didn't want money, just a guarantee that the movie wouldn't be made without him in the director's chair.

That proved to be an offer every studio in Hollywood could refuse, but fortunately, a couple of fellow Corman vets who had landed at Orion Pictures agreed to distribute the film if Corman and Hurd could find financing for its production. Enter Hemdale Films, a tiny production company run by John Daly, who offered to put up $4 million for *The Terminator*'s budget. Accustomed to working on a shoestring during his Corman days, Cameron agreed (although the final budget would end up closer to $6.5 million) and, with the assistance of Hurd and his boyhood friend William Wisher Jr., went to work on the screenplay.

The story of *The Terminator* was ingenious in its simplicity. Kyle Reese, a soldier from the year 2029, is sent back in time to 1984 in order to protect Sarah Connor, the mother of Reese's commanding officer in the War Against the Machines, John Connor. Sarah needs Reese's protection because the machines that rule the world in the post-apocalyptic future have sent their own soldier back in time—a cybernetic organism programmed to terminate Sarah and prevent John Connor from ever being born. What follows is a relentless chase, in the course of which a number of police officers and innocent bystanders are killed, and Sarah finds the inner strength to transform herself from waitress to warrior even as she and Kyle are falling in love. In the end, Sarah destroys the Terminator, but not before it kills Kyle Reese, the father of her unborn son, John.

With the screenplay completed, it was time for Cameron to cast his film. His first choice to play the Terminator was Lance Henriksen, an actor he'd worked with on *Piranha II.* (In fact, Henriksen had already given the role a test run by showing up for Cameron's pitch meeting at Hemdale with gold foil on his teeth and gruesome makeup on his face.) The studio countered with a bizarre casting suggestion: O. J. Simpson. Cameron, revealing the limits of his imagination, could not picture The Juice as a killer, nor could he stomach Orion's preferred choice for the role of Kyle Reese: Arnold Schwarzenegger. The director agreed to a lunch meeting with the *Conan* star, fully intending to sabotage it, but was instead charmed by Schwarzenegger. It eventually became clear that, although his agents were pushing him for the heroic role of Reese, the actor was much more captivated by the Terminator. Cameron had found his villain.

Henriksen was given the lesser role of a homicide detective investigating the Terminator's killing spree, while another actor Cameron had considered to play the cyborg, Michael Biehn, ended up with the part of Reese. Rounding out the main cast in the crucial role of Sarah Connor was Linda Hamilton, a relatively unknown actress Cameron felt could convey both the toughness and the vulnerability of the character. Filming was initially scheduled to begin in Toronto in the spring of 1983, when the production hit a snag: Dino de Laurentiis exercised an option he held on Schwarzenegger for a Conan sequel, and *The Terminator* was put on hold for a year while the actor shot *Conan the Destroyer*.

When filming finally began in March 1984, it was in downtown Los Angeles, not Toronto. Cameron's experience with Roger Corman paid off, as he was able to stick to a tight schedule, while shooting primarily at night. He recruited Stan Winston to create the special Terminator effects, including Schwarzenegger's makeup and a full-size mechanical puppet, while SFX shop Fantasy II contributed a stop-motion animated Terminator, as well as the futuristic battle scenes. After production wrapped in June, Cameron went into editing overdrive in order to deliver the film in time for its scheduled fall release.

Orion did little to publicize *The Terminator* before it hit theaters, which Cameron didn't appreciate, but the director had the last laugh when his film debuted at number one at the box office, ahead of such major studio releases as *Firstborn*, *Body Double*, and *American Dreamer*. The movie was no flash in the pan, either; it continued to rake in money through the Christmas season, surprising even Cameron by outgrossing high-profile holiday releases *Dune* and *2010*. Critics liked it, too, although their compliments were sometimes a bit backhanded. Writing in *The New York Times*, Janet Maslin called it "a B-movie with flair. Much of it, as directed by James Cameron (*Piranha II*), has suspense and personality, and only the obligatory mayhem becomes dull." *The Washington Post* called it a "slickly made, shoot-'em-up sci-fi fantasia" that "gleefully pillages everything from *The Forbin Project* to *Escape from the Planet of the Apes*, everyone from John Carpenter to Luis Bunuel." *Time* magazine named it one of the top ten movies of the year.

The Terminator's reputation has only improved in the decades since its release. Even the Library of Congress bestowed its seal of approval by inducting the film into its United States Film Registry in 2008. In comparison to most of the bloated, computer-generated blockbusters of today, the original *Terminator* remains a model of efficiency and ingenuity. It grabs you right from the opening crawl, with its declaration that the final battle between man and machine "will not be fought in the future—but tonight." Despite the poofy hairdos, goofy techno-pop tunes, and overabundance of MTV-pink neon, it doesn't feel dated, partly because of the plot's time-travel element. After all, the Terminator has been sent into the distant past of 1984 to complete its mission, and this is the mid-'80s as we remember them. It's true that the opening flash-forward scene, with its combination of scale models and front-screen projection, can't compare with the digital spectacle of the War Against the Machines as seen in 2009's *Terminator Salvation*, but it more than compensates for its modest budget with its old-school Corman-style flair.

The early scenes convey a sense of mystery and tension through neo-noir style; they're all rain-slicked city streets, crime-ridden alleyways, and police sirens wailing through the night. The shift to Sarah Connor's brightly lit "Bob's Big Boy" world is jarring, almost as if she's in a different movie—and at this point, she basically is. Only after the murders of the other Sarah Connors found in the phone book by the indiscriminate Terminator does she enter the film's dark, pre-apocalyptic world (at a club called "Tech Noir," a term that has since caught on as a descriptor of the sort of cyberpunk-tinged sci-fi/action movie *The Terminator* helped pioneer).

Perhaps because action movies have become so lumbering and unwieldy in recent years, *The Terminator* is often remembered as being lean, mean, and relentless—and that's true to a degree. There is a great deal of exposition, but as has often been noted, the backstory is pared down to its bare essentials, and most of it is delivered by Kyle Reese during high-speed car chases, so it doesn't slow the movie down much. But Cameron does slow things down in order to effectively develop the relationship between Connor and Reese, so it's not as if the film is simply nonstop mayhem. (I always think of it as one of the great up-all-night movies, like *After Hours* or *Dazed and Confused*; it wasn't until rewatching it for this introduction that I realized it actually takes place over three nights.) Despite the ongoing tension and moments of flat-out terror, there's no shortage of humor in the picture, much of it courtesy of Schwarzenegger's comic performance. Whether the former Mr. Universe *knew* he was giving a comic performance is a matter of debate—having seen the lamentable comedies in which he was trying to be funny, I suspect not—but even if James Cameron operated him like a puppet, there's no denying that Schwarzenegger invests the Terminator's robotic movements and minimal dialogue with wit and presence. Otherwise, how could a line as generic as "I'll be back" become one of the most quoted movie catchphrases of all time?

What stands out most of all when re-viewing *The Terminator* today, particularly in light of James Cameron's increasingly overwrought, years-in-the-making budget-busters, is the director's exuberant genre-bending panache. Seamlessly blending elements of science fiction, action, romance, film noir, war movies, slasher flicks, and creature features, *The Terminator* synthesizes nearly a century of cinema into 107 minutes of peerless pop entertainment. Cameron wears his influences on his sleeve, and that's what this book is all about: influences. In the pages ahead, we'll explore the films and television shows that helped inspire *The Terminator*, as well as those that have drawn inspiration from it. We'll delve into the history of science-fiction cinema, from its earliest days to the golden age of the 1950s and beyond, encountering killer robots, time travelers, and post-apocalyptic wastelands along the way. We'll trace the history of the *Terminator* franchise through its theatrical sequels, television series, comic books, novels, and videogames, and examine the "tech-noir" genre it helped spawn. We'll review the improbable career of Arnold Schwarzenegger, reevaluate the films of James Cameron, and find time along the way for some offbeat tangents as we dig deep into the hidden nooks and crannies of pop culture for the buried treasures within. From *Metropolis* to *The Matrix*, from *Frankenstein* to *RoboCop*, from H. G. Wells and Harlan Ellison to Roger Corman and Roland Emmerich, you'll find them all here . . . if you like *The Terminator*.

Klaatu: "The decision is made." (20th Century-Fox/Photofest)

1

PROTOTYPES: THE ROOTS OF SCIENCE-FICTION CINEMA

MAGICIANS OF THE SILENT AGE

Science fiction is a genre that's hard to pin down, but most of us think we know it when we see it. Sometimes it's easy to spot: rocket ships, flying saucers, little green men. Anything with a futuristic setting or an element of advanced technology is usually tagged with the sci-fi label, but the lines between genres often become blurred. If forced to choose only one or the other, would you describe *Alien* as a science-fiction movie or a horror movie? Sure, it has the trappings of sci-fi—it takes place in outer space, and there's an alien right there in the title—but it operates more like a haunted-house story. The goofy Matthew McConaughey flick *Reign of Fire* takes place in the future, but it involves dragons—so is it sci-fi or fantasy? And what about alternative histories, such as *Fatherland*, in which the Nazis won World War II? They aren't set in the future and don't involve advanced technology, so are they not science fiction?

The sci-fi genre attracts this sort of debate because its fans have a tendency toward the pedantic and nitpicky. Some of them don't even like the term *sci-fi*, preferring the much more dignified abbreviation "SF." In short, they are geeks, and fiercely proud of it. Given these circumstances, it would be foolhardy to attempt any kind of comprehensive definition of science fiction that would please everybody, so why even try? Let's just stick with "we know it when we see it," and we'll all get along famously.

Whatever your definition, one thing upon which we can all

agree is that the history of science-fiction movies dates back nearly as far as the history of cinema itself. In 1902, Georges Méliès wrote and directed the fourteen-minute short *A Trip to the Moon*, a seminal motion picture by any measure. A former stage magician, Méliès transferred his gifts for prestidigitation to the medium of film, creating an array of technical advances and special effects in the process. The story is primitive, although by the standards of the day it could be considered an epic narrative: A group of astronomers dressed like wizards decide to attempt a flight to the moon, using a bullet-shaped spaceship fired from an enormous cannon. They arrive safely, resulting in the film's most famous image, that of the spaceship lodged in the Man in the Moon's eye. From the moon's surface, they observe the Earth, Saturn, the stars, and snow, before entering a crater and discovering a crop of giant mushrooms, including one that sprouts from an umbrella opened by one of the astronomers. They are captured by the moon's inhabitants, known as Selenites, but are able to escape by pushing their spaceship off a cliff, allowing them to fall all the way to Earth and into the ocean. Yes, all of these things we now know to be scientifically accurate made their way into the Méliès film, making it all the more impressive as a historic artifact.

Okay, so the science in *A Trip to the Moon* may not have been airtight, but the groundbreaking effects, including animation, multiple exposures, superimpositions, and dissolves, proved enormously influential. But Méliès was not alone in experimenting with the whimsical possibilities of science fiction; British filmmaker Walter R. Booth was another magician who turned his talents to the nascent art of cinema. In Booth's 1906 short *The '?' Motorist*, a runaway automobile rides up the side of a building, flies into the clouds and around another smiley Moon, circles the rings of Saturn, and finally falls back to Earth, where it transforms into a horse and buggy. With its mix of model work and animation, Booth's 1909 effort *The Airship Destroyer* is an impressively prescient take on zeppelin-powered warfare, decades before World War II.

Many of the earliest attempts at filmed science fiction were adaptations of works by two of the genre's literary godfathers, Jules

Verne and H. G. Wells, including the first feature-length sci-fi film, 1916's *20,000 Leagues Under the Sea*. Directed by Stuart Paton, this early Universal release was actually cobbled together from two Verne novels, *20,000 Leagues* and *The Mysterious Island*. As a result, the plot ends up making very little sense, but, like many of today's blockbusters, the movie emphasizes special effects over storytelling. The Williamson brothers, "who alone have solved the secret of under-the-ocean photography," are shown taking a bow in the opening credits, and their innovative system of tubes and mirrors used to shoot far beneath the ocean's surface is indeed the film's main attraction. *20,000 Leagues* mostly plays like a primitive Jacques Cousteau documentary, but the undersea footage of divers hunting sharks is undeniably impressive for the time.

FRITZ LANG'S *METROPOLIS*

The earliest direct ancestor of *The Terminator*, and the fountainhead of all modern science-fiction cinema, is Fritz Lang's 1927 near-masterpiece *Metropolis*. A stunning technical achievement at the time of its release, *Metropolis* was the most expensive film of the silent era, a feast for the eyes fusing the styles of German Expressionism, Art Deco, and Futurism. The production design of Lang's film, with its towering skyscrapers, suspended highways and bridges, and industrial underworld, has influenced the look of films ranging from *Blade Runner* to *Brazil* to *Batman Returns*. As Lang told interviewer Gretchen Berg of *Cahiers du Cinéma* in 1965, *Metropolis* "was born from my first sight of the skyscrapers of New York in October, 1924 . . . The buildings seemed to be a vertical sail, scintillating and very light, a luxurious backdrop, suspended in the dark sky to dazzle, distract and hypnotize. At night, the city did not simply give the impression of living: it lived as illusions lived."

The story of *Metropolis*, concocted by Lang and his wife Thea von Harbou, concerns a dystopian society of the future, in which the wealthy leisure class lives a life of luxury in opulent towers, while the workers toil below the earth to keep the machines that power the city running. Freder, the son of the city's founder Fredersen, falls for the saintly Maria, who preaches her message of brotherhood and love to the workers. Detecting the rumblings of revolution, Fredersen conspires with mad scientist Rotwang, a former romantic rival, who has built a humanoid and distinctly feminine robot. Rotwang disguises the machine as Maria and sends it below, not to quell the worker resistance as Fredersen instructed, but to sow further discord between those underground and their oppressors. A riot breaks out and the city's plumbing system is destroyed, causing massive flooding and the near-drowning of the workers' children before they are rescued by Maria and Freder. The robot Maria is burned at the stake, while the real one joins with Freder to mediate peace and understanding between management and labor.

It's a simplistic, often sentimental narrative, one that Lang doesn't exactly execute in a crisp and dexterous manner, and the hyperemotive performances are over the top even by the standards of the silent era. But *Metropolis* has endured because of its sumptuous visuals and groundbreaking special effects. It would be an oversimplification to say it was all done with mirrors—Lang and his team did construct massive sets for the film—but many of the effects combining actors with miniatures and models were achieved using mirrors placed at angles to the camera. Long shots of automobiles and planes moving through the city required a painstaking stop-motion process, while more traditional lighting and in-camera effects were utilized for the transformation of the robot into Maria. Lang's most startling innovation may have been the use of subjective camera during the machine explosion—an effect that, as Lang put it, "gave the public the impression that the two actors actually felt the shock."

Metropolis was not particularly well received in its day. It was heavily reedited following its Berlin premiere in January 1927, with more than a half hour trimmed from its 150-minute running time. (The film was not restored to something approaching its original form until 2008, when a 16mm print of the Berlin premiere cut was discovered in Argentina.) H. G. Wells famously eviscerated *Metropolis* in a *New York Times* review, writing, "I have recently seen the silliest film. I do not believe it would be possible to make one sillier . . . Originality there is none. Independent thought, none . . . I do not think there is a single new idea, a single instance of artistic creation or even intelligent anticipation, from first to last in the whole pretentious stew." Even Fritz Lang gave his own creation the cold shoulder later in life, telling Peter Bogdanovich in 1965, "I didn't like the picture—thought it was silly and stupid . . . should I say now that I like *Metropolis* because something I have seen in my imagination comes true, when I detested it after it was finished?"

The film's reputation has improved greatly over the years—it even survived an ill-advised 1984 re-release supervised by Giorgio Morodor, who replaced the original score with an array of ghastly pop tunes by the likes of Billy Squier and Loverboy—and its influence on the science-fiction genre in general and *The Terminator* in particular can't be overstated. In addition to the theme of a human uprising against a mechanized society, *Metropolis* arguably features the first movie robot (although cases can be made for several comedic shorts, including *The Electric Servant* and *A Mechanical Husband*), and certainly the first that is made to look human in order to infiltrate the populace. It's unlikely that anyone has ever cited Brigitte Helm as an acting influence on Arnold Schwarzenegger, but like the later Terminator, Helm found the humor in her mechanical character's body language. (Let's hope she was trying to be at least a *little* funny in the scene wherein the robot Maria whips the men of Metropolis into a slavering frenzy with her hoochie-coochie moves.) And when she incites the workers to rise up against the devices that feed on their flesh and blood with a cry of "Death to the machines!" we might well be looking at a silent-era Sarah Connor.

Given its exorbitant cost and dismal box-office performance, it's no surprise that *Metropolis* did not exactly trigger a wave of ambitious, big-budget science-fiction filmmaking. Rare exceptions, such as the 1930 musical *Just Imagine*, set in the far-off futuristic year of 1980 ("when everyone has a number instead of a name, and the government tells you whom you should marry") and 1936's prescient H. G. Wells–scripted British epic *Things to Come*, failed to connect with large audiences. Instead, Depression-era moviegoers embraced pulpy serials—cheaply made comic strips come to life, such as Buster Crabbe in *Buck Rogers* and *Flash Gordon Conquers the Universe*. But this was also the era of the Universal monsters, and while most movie buffs would categorize *Dracula*, *The Mummy*, *The Wolf Man*, and their sequels as horror films, the most popular creature in the Universal fold had one foot in the science-fiction genre—and a huge influence on *The Terminator*.

THE MODERN PROMETHEUS

Published in 1818, Mary Shelley's *Frankenstein* is considered by many to be the first science-fiction novel. It had been adapted for the screen once before, in a 1910 short from Edison Studios, before James Whale directed the classic version for Universal in 1931. Owing more to a theatrical adaptation of Shelley's book by Peggy Webling than to the novel itself, Whale's film told the story of Dr. Henry Frankenstein, a grave-robbing scientist with a God complex who stitches various purloined body parts (along with the brain of a criminal obtained by his somewhat less than competent hunchbacked assistant, Fritz) into an iconic movie monster. Bela Lugosi had originally been cast as the creature, but after a failed makeup test, the role went to Boris Karloff. (Lugosi would eventually play the monster in 1943's *Frankenstein Meets the Wolf Man*.)

Karloff's fearsome yet empathetic performance, along with Whale's atmospheric, Gothic take on the material (as filtered through German Expressionism), transformed an ordinary creature feature into an American classic. Although the monster has been reimagined many times over the last eight decades, any mention of the name "Frankenstein" will forever conjure the image of Karloff, complete with flattop and neck bolts. Even under all the makeup, the actor was able to connect with some buried core of humanity within the abomination and make the audience feel for this violent, murderous creation.

As Sean French writes in his slim but invaluable BFI Modern Classics volume on *The Terminator*, "Schwarzenegger's terminator demands to be compared with one of the mythic creations of the cinema, Boris Karloff's great performance as Frankenstein's monster in James Whale's 1931 film." The resemblance is more physical than emotional, as the Terminator is completely devoid of humanity and Schwarzenegger never makes a play for our empathy. But he's certainly built like Frankenstein's monster, and as the Terminator deteriorates throughout the course of the movie (particularly once he's been burned by the exploding gasoline truck), he takes on more and more of a resemblance to Karloff's classic creature. In a sense, both characters are born from a bolt of lightning; the monster literally so, as Dr. Frankenstein uses the electrical charge from a lightning storm to bring his creation to life, but don't forget that the Terminator's first appearance is accompanied by a burst of blue lightning as he arrives from the future.

There are some less obvious parallels, as well. These roles were star-making and career-defining for both actors; Karloff's name didn't even appear in the opening credits to *Frankenstein*, as the role of the monster was attributed simply to "?" Both men reprised their roles in sequels, by which time they had become much bigger stars. For *The Bride of Frankenstein* (1935), also directed by Whale, Karloff was given the full above-the-title treatment, no first name necessary, in much the same way that many a movie poster and videotape box of the '80s and '90s bore the name "Schwarzenegger" in large banner letters. Both the monster and the Terminator were made more lovable in their second appearance, and both were given much more dialogue than in the original. (In Karloff's case, this was easily done, as he didn't speak at all in *Frankenstein*, but even Schwarzenegger had only sixteen lines of dialogue in his first go-round as the Terminator.) And both actors would eventually see their franchises carry on without them.

THE GOLDEN AGE OF SCIENCE FICTION

Science fiction did not come into its own as an American movie genre until after World War II, but when it arrived, it hit with the impact of a nuclear blast. All of a nation's anxieties about atomic energy coalesced into a wave of motion pictures that transformed those fears into nail-biting entertainment. "All science fiction is this kind of dualistic dance, love–hate relationship with technology," said James Cameron on the Turner Classic Movies special *Watch the Skies*. "You know, a nuclear bomb can destroy us, but a nuclear-powered spaceship can take us to the stars."

The 1950 George Pal production *Destination Moon* was not particularly beloved by Cameron, but it was an important step in the evolution of the science-fiction film, depicting space travel in a realistic fashion for the first time. It was also the launchpad for a cinematic golden age of science fiction, which blasted into orbit the following year with the release of two all-time classics of the genre, offering two different takes on the arrival of visitors from the stars, *The Day the Earth Stood Still* and *The Thing from Another World.*

In *The Day the Earth Stood Still*, directed by Robert Wise, the alien arrives bearing gifts, but the U.S. military shoots first and asks questions later. The space ambassador known as Klaatu (Michael Rennie) is wounded when a soldier mistakes his present for a weapon, at which point Klaatu's own terminator of sorts, the imposing robot Gort, vaporizes all of the actual weapons in the area. Klaatu has a message for all humanity, but in order to properly deliver it, he first disguises himself as an ordinary human and seeks the assistance of one of the era's top scientists. The visitor's message is one of peace—or else. If mankind's warlike ways extend beyond the planet to the stars, the Earth will be destroyed.

The Thing is in many ways the inverse of *The Day the Earth Stood Still.* The alien discovered frozen near an Arctic research base is closer to vegetable than man, and offers no warnings before embarking on a destructive rampage. While *Day* portrayed the military as trigger-happy and the men of science as our hope for the future, *The Thing* has no time for such high-minded ideals. It's clear all along that the scientists who want to keep the creature alive are pompous eggheads and that the shoot-first G.I. Joes have the right idea. As Stephen King puts it in *Danse Macabre*, his survey of the horror genre, "*The Thing* is the first movie of the fifties to offer us the scientist in the role of the Appeaser, that creature who for reasons either craven or misguided, would open the gates to the Garden of Eden and let all the evils fly in." That's a sci-fi trope that endured, and certainly one that informs the *Terminator* series, in which all scientists are suspect and any of them might be responsible for bringing on the end of the world. (Another tidbit Cameron may have picked up from *The Thing*: the dogs going crazy whenever the creature draws near.)

The military-vs.-science dynamic arises again in 1953's *War of the Worlds*, but this time religion is added to the mix. Loosely based on the H. G. Wells novel, this George Pal production took *The Thing*'s modest alien invasion and amplified it into a Technicolor spectacle. In many ways, *War of the Worlds* was the precursor of the blockbuster age; it featured groundbreaking special effects, nearly continuous action, and a global scope that would be oft imitated in decades to come. When the Martian invaders level the Eiffel Tower, it's hard not to think of the destruction of the White House decades later in *Independence Day* and the whole wave of "disaster porn" that followed.

At first it seems religion gets the short of end of the stick in the battle to save humanity, as a priest who approaches the Martian war machine is instantly vaporized. The military solution is predictable and unsuccessful, as the alien force fields prove impervious to nuclear weapons. It seems it's up to science to find a solution in the form of biological warfare—as in the novel, the invaders have no resistance to earthbound germs that are harmless to humans—but the film presents this deus ex machina as an almost literal act of God, as the Martians are felled by disease just as the desperate masses of humanity gather in a church to pray for divine intervention. It's not too much of a stretch to see this particular *War of the Worlds* as a metaphor for the war against the godless Communists.

By 1956, when Don Siegel's original version of *Invasion of the Body Snatchers* was released, Cold War paranoia had given rise to McCarthyism. No one could have made a straightforward movie on the subject without being blacklisted, so as was increasingly becoming the trend, the science-fiction genre was used as cover. In place of Commies, Siegel deployed spores from outer space that sprouted into exact duplicates of the residents of a small American town. Could your neighbor, someone you've known all your life, actually be plotting your destruction? Those were the fears of the day, but none of that subtext is necessary to appreciate Siegel's noir-ish sci-fi horror. Anyone who watched it as a child and then spent a week lying awake at night worried that Mom and Dad had been replaced by evil aliens can tell you that. When Kevin McCarthy finally snaps and spills the whole story to a psychiatrist in a speech that's indistinguishable from a delusional paranoid rant, the precedent is set for Sarah Connor's similar showdown with Earl Boen's Dr. Silberman in *Terminator 2*.

Of all the movies that made up Hollywood's golden age of science fiction, none has proved more influential than 1956's *Forbidden Planet*. As Cameron recalls on the TCM documentary included on the film's DVD release, "*Forbidden Planet* is an amazing film. It was amazing as a technical accomplishment in its day, just for its scope, just for the scale of its imagination." The movie's depiction of a militarized space exploration fleet (here led by straitlaced Leslie Nielsen, decades before his self-parodying heyday) planted the seeds for some of the biggest science-fiction franchises of all time, including *Star Trek* and *Star Wars*. And the supporting player affectionately dubbed Robby the Robot became a cultural icon, firmly establishing the concept of the robot in the popular consciousness. Robby's movie career was short-lived, as he came in toward the end of the golden age, but he would go on to make a number of appearances in a fruitful new frontier for science fiction: television.

FIVE NON–SCIENCE FICTION MOVIES THAT INFLUENCED *THE TERMINATOR*

1. *Halloween* (1978)—You could peg any number of early John Carpenter films as influences on *The Terminator* and you probably wouldn't be wrong. Carpenter's student-film-turned-feature *Dark Star* goofs on the theme of technology turning on its human creators. The Terminator's attack on the police station where Kyle Reese and Sarah Connor are being held recalls *Assault on Precinct 13*. And with its dark, dystopian city of the future, *Escape from New York* (on which Cameron worked as a matte artist and director of photography for special visual effects) can be seen as an early adopter of the tech-noir aesthetic. But it's Carpenter's creepy tale of a nearly unstoppable killer, with its frequent use of first-person camera from the villain's point of view, that had the most profound impact on *The Terminator*.

2. *Das Boot* (1981)—The future glimpsed in *The Terminator* is not one of gleaming corridors and shiny metallic surfaces, but a decaying world of rust and clanky, outmoded technology. *The Road Warrior* was the primary influence for this post-apocalyptic vision, but a less obvious antecedent is this World War II picture directed by Wolfgang Petersen. As Sean French notes in his BFI *Terminator* volume, the German U-boat "in the war film Cameron so admired . . . is not gleamingly solid, but rattling, rickety, leaking, dirty."

3. *The Driver* (1978)—In an early interview, Cameron says that he "had *The Driver* in mind when I was writing certain scenes in *The Terminator*. Not that I was cribbing; I had only seen the picture once and just had a dim memory of the kinetic forward energy." His memory is spot-on, as Walter Hill's minimalist tale of a taciturn getaway driver (Ryan O'Neal) trying to pull off a big score under the nose of a dogged cop (Bruce Dern) hums with some of the most visceral chase sequences ever filmed. Hill's use of the night streets of Los Angeles definitely made an impression on Cameron.

4. *Un Chien Andalou* (1929)—This surreal collaboration between Luis Buñuel and Salvador Dalí is admittedly an unlikely source of inspiration for an '80s action movie starring Arnold Schwarzenegger. A silent, black-and-white sixteen-minute short, *Andalou* is a free-floating chain of disturbing imagery, including an army of ants emerging from a man's palm, a woman poking a severed hand with a cane, and a pair of dead donkeys draped over grand pianos. But the film's most notorious image, that of a man slashing a woman's eye with a straight razor, is explicitly referenced when the Terminator cuts out his own damaged eyeball.

5. *In a Lonely Place* (1950)—Cameron has never actually cited Nicholas Ray's classic L.A. noir as an influence on *The Terminator*, but in naming the nightclub in his film Tech Noir, he's clearly tipping his fedora to those grim, shadowy films of the '40s and '50s, and his depiction of the seedy night world of Los Angeles certainly owes a debt to the genre. Any number of examples could take this spot on the list, but Ray's haunting tale of a cynical screenwriter (Humphrey Bogart) accused of murder is one of the best.

SCI-FI SCHLOCK: SO BAD THEY'RE GOOD

Sure, the golden age of science fiction produced its share of timeless classics . . . but it also inspired some of the looniest space cadets in motion-picture history to make movies that nearly defy description. Goofy concepts combined with microscopic budgets and technical ineptitude proved to be a popular recipe throughout the '50s and early '60s, resulting in plenty of future fodder for *Mystery Science Theater 3000*. But you won't need wisecracking robots to help keep you amused while watching any of these jaw-dropping, mind-warping crimes against cinema:

***Plan 9 from Outer Space* (1959)**—"Greetings, my friend. We are all interested in the future, for that is where you and I are going to spend the rest of our lives." With those fateful words, Edward D. Wood Jr. launched his disasterpiece, destined to go down in the annals of motion picture history as the worst movie ever made. *Plan 9* is best known for Bela Lugosi's last film appearance (Lugosi died and was replaced by a chiropractor holding a cape over his face), but it's Wood's naive belief in his vision of aliens resurrecting the Earth's dead that makes this insanely inept endeavor the most beloved bad movie of all time.

***Robot Monster* (1953)**—Forget everything you think you know about robot monsters—unless you think they look like men in gorilla suits wearing diving helmets, in which case, you're right on director Phil Tucker's wavelength. Having destroyed all human life on Earth except for a German professor and his wife, his shirtless assistant, and his annoying children, Ro-Man Extension XJ-9 too late comes to the realization that what he really wants is "to be like the humans. To laugh, feel, want." A deserving Golden Turkey Award winner.

***The Brain That Wouldn't Die* (1962)**—This bonkers *Frankenstein* riff concerns an arrogant surgeon whose experimental transplanting techniques are put to the test after his girlfriend is decapitated in a car accident. After reaching into the burning wreckage and carefully rolling his beloved's severed head up in his jacket, he brings it to his country estate, where he already has one stitched-together abomination locked in a closet. Our man of science then does what any red-blooded American male would do: he heads down to the nearest strip joint to find a new body for his girlfriend. Rest assured that the hubris of this man who would play God does not go unpunished.

***The Beast of Yucca Flats* (1961)**—Like many of the finest science-fiction films of the era, *The Beast of Yucca Flats* is a cautionary tale about our atomic age. Unlike many of the finest science-fiction films of the era, it features Swedish wrestler Tor Johnson as a Russian scientist transformed into a murderous mutant by a nuclear blast. Johnson, a veteran of three Ed Wood pictures, must have felt right at home on the set of this no-budget dud, which was shot with no sound equipment whatsoever. Instead, the story is told through meandering and often irrelevant narration—during a low-speed car chase the narrator muses, "Flag on the Moon. How did it get there?"—and occasional poorly dubbed dialogue whenever the characters' faces are hidden from the camera.

***Santa Claus Conquers the Martians* (1964)**—For some reason, this yuletide tale of Kris Kringle's abduction by aliens never caught on as a perennial holiday classic like *The Grinch Who Stole Christmas*. Perhaps the notion of Santa permanently relocating to the red planet was too frightening for small children to bear. Or maybe the film's anti-technology message, expressed through Santa's dissatisfaction with a fully automated and easily sabotaged workshop, was simply out of step with the changing times. But it's most likely because the Styrofoam sets, tinfoil robots, and indifferently applied green Martian makeup suggested an abdication of responsibility at the most basic level of craftsmanship.

Jill Haworth and David McCallum in *The Outer Limits*: "There is nothing wrong with your television set. Do not attempt to adjust the picture." (ABC-TV/Photofest)

2

DO NOT ATTEMPT TO ADJUST THE PICTURE: *THE OUTER LIMITS*

PLEASE STAND BY

The 1950s may have been a golden age for science fiction at the movies, but the same could not be said for the small screen. Anyone hoping to get a sci-fi fix from television had to settle for kiddie shows like *Captain Video and His Video Rangers* or *Tom Corbett, Space Cadet*. The anthology shows of the day might make an occasional foray into the genre, but otherwise, those longing for something a bit more sophisticated than men in tinfoil helmets and longjohns shooting rayguns were out of luck. That changed somewhat when Rod Serling brought *The Twilight Zone* into American living rooms in 1959, but thoughtful science fiction didn't get a full-fledged showcase on the prime-time schedule until producer Leslie Stevens teamed with writer Joseph Stefano for *The Outer Limits*.

Running for two seasons and forty-nine episodes on ABC, *The Outer Limits* began life in 1963 as a pilot called *Please Stand By*. With his company Daystar Productions, Stevens had enjoyed limited success at the network with the one-season rodeo series *Stoney Burke* starring Jack Lord, as well as a slew of failed spinoff pilots. After Daystar produced *Please Stand By*, which became the *Outer Limits* premiere episode "The Galaxy Being," Stevens decided he needed a partner to help shoulder the burden of the series to come—preferably someone with a reputation that would make selling the idea to sponsors an easier task. He approached Stefano, a songwriter-turned-screenwriter best known for adapting Robert Bloch's novel *Psycho* for Alfred Hitchcock.

Stevens and Stefano assembled an impressive team for the series, particularly on the technical end. Future three-time Academy Award winner Conrad Hall served as director of photography on many episodes, assisted by William Fraker, who would himself go on to be nominated for six Oscars. One young viewer who was impressed by the look of the show was James Cameron. "The thing that *The Outer Limits* had, that always impressed me visually, was its use of the deep focus *film noir* look of the '40s films and the German Expressionist movies of the '30s," he told *Cinefantastique* in 1985. (And as we'll soon see, that was not the only admission he made about *The Outer Limits.*)

At the network's insistence, each episode of the series would feature a monster of the week, which came to be known as "the bear." According to *The Outer Limits: The Official Companion*, Stefano explained the bear thusly: "In the days of vaudeville, when things were going wrong and the audience was getting bored, out would come a comic in a bear outfit. Or a trained bear. That's what we do in each of our shows—we bring on the bear!" As a result of this mandate, the makeup artists and costume designers worked overtime churning out a number of memorable (and often gruesome) "bears," including David McCallum as a bulbous-headed man of the future in "The Sixth Finger" and Martin Landau as a mutant remnant of humanity in "The Man Who Was Never Born." But *The Outer Limits* is probably best remembered for its eerie opening narration delivered by "The Control Voice":

> *There is nothing wrong with your television set. Do not attempt to adjust the picture. We are controlling transmission . . . We will control the horizontal. We will control the vertical . . . For the next hour, sit quietly and we will control all that you see and hear. We repeat: there is nothing wrong with your television set. You are about to participate in a great adventure. You are about to experience the awe and mystery which reaches from the inner mind to . . . The Outer Limits.*

The show's first season was successful enough to secure a renewal, although it was bumped from its Monday-night slot to Saturdays, usually a harbinger of doom, particularly since it would be going up against the very popular *Jackie Gleason Show*. Angered by the move, Stefano quit the series and was replaced by producer Ben Brady. For many viewers, the resulting truncated second season was a disappointment, although at least two of its episodes would come to be regarded as among the series' best.

ENTER ELLISON

One viewer who wasn't particularly impressed with the first season of *The Outer Limits* was an outspoken young science-fiction writer named Harlan Ellison, who thought it was "garbage, the usual monster bullshit. They were doing the 'bear on the beach,' in which you open with a bear on a beach, then you ask *how* the bear got on the beach. It was a lot of funny rubber masks, and basically silly ideas." Ellison had broken into television writing for shows like *Burke's Law* and *Voyage to the Bottom of the Sea*, on which he'd made a lasting impression by attacking an ABC executive in mid-meeting, causing the exec to break his pelvis when a model of the series' submarine, *Seaview*, fell on him.

New *Outer Limits* producer Ben Brady apparently wasn't too worried about Ellison attacking him in a meeting, as he hired him to pen the second-season opener, "Soldier." He was pleased enough with the results to bring Ellison back for a second episode, "Demon with a Glass Hand," later that season. Shortly thereafter, the series was canceled, and Ellison moved on to other television work, little dreaming that his *Outer Limits* scripts would become the center of controversy two decades later.

"Some years ago, before *The Terminator* came out, I began to hear from people, 'Gee, there's this script that they're going to shoot that reads an awful lot like your script for 'Soldier' that you did on *Outer Limits* years ago," Ellison said in an interview for TV Ontario's *Prisoners of Gravity*. "So we applied to Hemdale Films for a copy of the script, and they refused to let us see it. . . . Well, as an accredited film critic in Hollywood, I see every film, and I get a screening pass to every film. We did not get one to *Terminator*." Nonetheless, Ellison did get into a press screening by posing as Leonard Maltin's assistant. He enjoyed the movie, writing in his "Harlan Ellison's Watching" column in *The Magazine of Fantasy and Science Fiction* that it was "a superlative piece of work and deserves its success . . . The film is taut, memorable, and clearly based on brilliant source material." In case there was any ambiguity about that last cheeky statement, he added, "As I write this, attorneys are talking."

He expanded upon this commentary in his *Prisoners of Gravity* interview. "The editors of *Starlog* magazine called me and said, 'We're getting a lot of heat all of a sudden from James Cameron and Gale Anne Hurd' . . . What had happened was, they had interviewed Cameron prior to the film's release . . . and in the course of this interview, someone had said to him, 'Where did you get the basic conception for *Terminator*?' And his response was, oh, I ripped off a couple of *Outer Limits* segments." That quote didn't appear in the published issue of *Starlog*, but Ellison had friends at the magazine who slipped him a copy of the original transcript. He also had a friend named Tracy Tormé, a screenwriter who had been on the set of *The Terminator*. "He was talking to Cameron, and he said 'Where did you get the idea for this?' And Cameron said 'Oh, I ripped off a couple of Ellison's short stories and a couple of Ellison's *Outer Limits* segments.'"

Ellison and his lawyers took their findings to Hemdale and Orion, and an out-of-court settlement was reached. Compared to the massive profits the *Terminator* franchise has raked in over the years, his financial windfall wasn't much: somewhere in the $65,000–75,000 range. But more important to the writer, the agreement also stipulated that a credit be added to the film for every re-release, re-broadcast, video or DVD edition, stating simply: "Acknowledgment to the works of Harlan Ellison." Cameron, for his part, was not happy with the settlement. "It was a nuisance suit that could easily have been fought," he said, according to Rebecca Keegan's biography *The Futurist*. "I expected Hemdale and Orion to fight for my rights, but they abandoned me . . . I had no choice but to agree to the settlement. Of course, there was a gag order, as well, so I couldn't tell this story, but now I frankly don't care. Harlan Ellison is a parasite who can kiss my ass."

Looking back on it now, it certainly seems as though Cameron had every right to be upset. Ellison's first *Outer Limits* episode, the second-season premiere "Soldier," opens with a battle scene set against a blighted futuristic backdrop, as does *The Terminator*. Two enemy combatants are hit with light rays that send them into a swirling time vortex. One soldier becomes stuck between two times, while the other, Qarlo, arrives in our present, in a city alleyway, where he is confronted by a police officer—much as Kyle Reese would be in Cameron's film. (Ellison probably should have sued himself for plagiarism, as well, since he reused this scene in his *Star Trek* episode "The City on the Edge of Forever," another story of future soldiers traveling to the past to ensure the death of an influential woman.)

Once Qarlo is captured by the authorities, any similarity between the *Outer Limits* episode and *The Terminator* ceases to exist. A linguist named Kagan determines that Qarlo is speaking a variation on English, and he is eventually able to deduce that the soldier comes from Earth's future. Kagan attempts to domesticate Qarlo by bringing him home to stay with him and his family, but his efforts are fruitless. Qarlo knows only war, and before long he has broken into a gun shop to secure a new weapon. When his enemy from the future becomes unstuck in time, the two warriors are finally reunited in battle, at which point they disappear in another flash of light.

Similarly, the second Ellison episode of *Outer Limits*, "Demon with a Glass Hand," concerns another man of the future sent back to our time in an effort to save humanity. This is Trent (Robert Culp), who has been pursued through the time mirror by the Kyben, a race of aliens bent on exterminating mankind. Trent is equipped with a translucent computerized hand that's missing several fingers, so that for the first half of the episode he appears to be making the heavy metal "devil horns" sign. As he tracks down and installs the remaining fingers, the hand's power grows, until it is able to reveal to him what has happened to the 70 billion people who vanished from his future Earth. They have all been digitized and stored on a wire inside him—for as Trent learns at episode's end, he is not a man, but a robot.

Again, there are elements here that also turn up in *The Terminator*—time travel, a robot in human form, an apocalyptic future—but these are all tried-and-true science-fiction tropes, none of which were created by Harlan Ellison. This is not to say that Cameron was not inspired by Ellison's work; he clearly was. But as we have already seen (and will continue to see in the chapters ahead), Cameron was inspired by the efforts of many other writers and filmmakers, as well. The charge of plagiarism seems especially overheated from a twenty-first-century perspective, as so many of today's artists, filmmakers, and musicians are unabashed about borrowing elements from our shared pop culture and building on what has come before. If James Cameron is a plagiarist, what does that make Quentin Tarantino? Or Kanye West? At worst, Cameron is guilty of sampling, which is hardly a crime in the current artistic landscape. (Still, this would not be the last time Cameron faced accusations of plagiarism, as we shall see later in these pages.)

What makes this whole controversy especially absurd is that the story of *The Terminator* is more indebted to an *Outer Limits* episode Ellison didn't even write than it is to either "Soldier" or "Demon with a Glass Hand." In the first-season episode "The Man Who Was Never Born," an astronaut named Reardon passes through a "time convulsion" on his return to Earth and arrives to find it's the twenty-second century and the planet is a wasteland. He meets a mutant named Andro (Martin Landau), who informs him that most of humanity was wiped out centuries ago by a biological catastrophe caused by a man named Bertram Cabot Jr. Reardon takes Andro with him as he attempts to return to his own time; the effort is successful, but Reardon is killed in the process. Disguising himself as a normal human, Andro attempts to track down and kill Bertram Cabot Jr., but it turns out he has yet to be born. Instead, Andro realizes that that the woman he has fallen for is destined to become the mother of this man who must never exist. Flip-flop a couple of the details, and you can see the similarity to *The Terminator*'s plot, yet episode writer Anthony Lawrence never sued Cameron—and there's certainly no "acknowledgment to the works of Anthony Lawrence" in the *Terminator* credits.

After an abbreviated second season of seventeen episodes, *The Outer Limits* returned control of your television for the last time on January 16, 1965. In a sense, though, the show never really left the airwaves, living on in nearly continuous syndication and growing in popularity throughout the '60s and '70s. In the mid-'80s, Stevens and Stefano were approached by ABC about a possible revival of the show, but nothing came of it. Finally, in 1995, a new version of *The Outer Limits* debuted on Showtime, with Stevens and Stefano serving as consultants. It ran for seven seasons, producing more than three times the number of episodes as the original series but not even a fraction of its cultural impact.

FIVE ESSENTIAL *OUTER LIMITS* EPISODES (NOT WRITTEN BY HARLAN ELLISON)

"The Architects of Fear"—James Cameron can at least console himself with the knowledge that he's not the only writer to ever draw inspiration from *The Outer Limits*. Comic-book author Alan Moore famously swiped the climax of his acclaimed *Watchmen* series from this episode about a group of scientists who stage an alien invasion in order to bring about world peace.

"The Sixth Finger"—David McCallum displays remarkable range as a Welsh miner who participates in an experiment that transforms him into a super-intelligent man of the future in this chilling first-season episode.

"A Feasibility Study"—In an episode that may have influenced later tech-noir efforts such as *Dark City*, the inhabitants of a small town wake up one morning to find their entire village has been transported to an alien world. The aliens are conducting a study to see whether humans will make an effective slave labor force, and the actions of the ordinary people of this town will determine whether the entire population of Earth is enslaved.

"The Forms of Things Unknown"—One of the strangest hours in television history, at least until *Twin Peaks* reached the airwaves in the early '90s, this episode concerning blackmail, murder, and time travel is notable not so much for its plot, but for its eerie style, which bears a closer resemblance to '60s art films by Ingmar Bergman and Roman Polanski than to anything else on American TV at the time.

"The Inheritors"—One of the few second-season entries to match the quality of season one, this two-part episode stars Robert Duvall as a government agent investigating four soldiers imbued with extraordinary powers after contact with an alien intelligence. The gradual unveiling of the soldiers' bizarre project, and the mystery surrounding their motives, will keep you guessing to the end.

OTHER HARLAN ELLISON CONTROVERSIES

It must be exhausting to be Harlan Ellison. He is a man who suffers no fools, and by his own admission, nearly everything makes him angry. "I'm just a hard pill to swallow," he says in the engaging 2008 documentary *Harlan Ellison: Dreams with Sharp Teeth*. "If you had to live with me 24/7, you'd put a gun in either your mouth or my mouth." Says his friend Neil Gaiman (*Sandman, American Gods*), he's "a huge piece of performance art called Harlan Ellison." In a career spanning more than half a century, Ellison has butted heads with publishers, motion picture and television producers, fellow writers, and fans. Delving into his various feuds, lawsuits, and vendettas is like peeling the layers of an onion, so in the interest of keeping this sidebar to a manageable length, here is just a sampling of the controversies Harlan Ellison has been involved in over the years.

Ellison vs. Star Trek—The Ellison-scripted "City on the Edge of Forever" is routinely described as the best episode *Star Trek* ever produced, but such accolades are cold comfort for the writer, who vented his spleen in the 1996 introduction to a published edition of his original screenplay. That version of the script won a Writer's Guild Award after the episode aired in 1967, but as *Trek* fans are well aware, Ellison's "City" was oft rewritten, initially by him, but finally by members of the *Trek* writing staff. Over the years, *Trek* creator Gene Roddenberry took many shots at Ellison, claiming the script could not be filmed as written on the show's budget and, more dubiously, that Ellison's version featured the popular character Scotty selling drugs on the USS *Enterprise*. That's clearly not true, as the published edition shows, and in the introduction Ellison eviscerates the now-deceased Great Bird of the Galaxy in excruciating detail. More recently, Ellison sued Paramount over royalties from merchandise derived from "City on the Edge of Forever," including the "Crucible" trilogy of *Star Trek* novels and a Guardian of Forever talking Christmas tree ornament. The matter was settled out of court.

Ellison vs. Fantagraphics—At one time, Ellison and this respected comic book publisher were allies, linked as co-defendants in a libel suit over comments Ellison made in an interview with Fantagraphics publication *The Comics Journal*. (He had referred to writer Mike Fleisher as "derange-o" and "bugfuck," but of course, in Ellison's world, those are intended as compliments.) The defendants prevailed, but their relationship was damaged; Fantagraphics owner Gary Groth often took potshots at Ellison in the pages of *The Comics Journal*, and in 1996 he published *The Book on the Edge of Forever*, which was highly critical of Ellison. (More on that follows.) For his part, Ellison called Groth a cockroach, a bum, and "one of the most evil, mean-spirited, rotten little human beings I've ever met" at a comic book convention in 1993. The straw that broke the camel's back was an excerpt from *Comics as Art: We Told You So*, a still-unpublished history of Fantagraphics that ran on the company's website. "Being a co-defendant with Ellison made me feel like I was in the Alamo: surrounded on all sides," Groth is quoted as saying. "He was always coming up with schemes to wheedle out of paying his bills." Ellison filed a lawsuit against Fantagraphics for defamation (ironic, considering how all this had started), a case that was settled with both parties agreeing to speak no further evil of each other. Easier said than done.

Ellison vs. The Last Dangerous Visions—In 1967 Doubleday published one of the most acclaimed short-story anthologies of all time, *Dangerous Visions*. The editor of this volume was one Harlan Ellison, who encouraged the contributing writers to push the boundaries of what was considered acceptable in the field of science fiction. In other words, it was a '60s thing, dealing in not only sex, drugs, and rock 'n' roll, but in civil unrest, the Vietnam War, and other taboos of the era. The collection was such a success, it was followed by a sequel, *Again, Dangerous Visions*, in 1972. In that book's introduction, Ellison announced that a third volume, *The Last Dangerous Visions*, was to follow, "God willing, approximately six months after this book." As it turns out, God was not willing. Nearly forty years later, the collection has still not appeared. As documented by Christopher Priest in *The Book on the Edge of Forever*, the intervening decades have seen Ellison announce numerous publication dates, switch publishers several times, and continue to add new stories to what would be a mammoth three-volume set if ever completed. Many of the contributors are long since dead, and those who have asked for their stories back have suffered the wrath of Ellison, according to Priest's account (backed up by letters from several participants). As late as 2007, Ellison was still hoping to finish the project, telling Newsarama.com, "It's this giant Sisyphean rock that I have to keep rolling up a hill, and people will not stop bugging me about it."

Ellison vs. In Time—Time seemed to loop back on itself in a very Ellisonian fashion in September 2011, when the author filed suit against distributor New Regency, claiming their science-fiction film *In Time* ripped off his short story "Repent, Harlequin! Said the Ticktockman." According to the author, the film by writer/director Andrew Niccol (*Gattaca*) bore an uncomfortable resemblance to his tale of "a dystopian corporate future in which everyone is allotted a specific amount of time to live." Ellison had a rare change of heart, however, withdrawing the lawsuit after the film starring Justin Timberlake and Amanda Seyfried opened to poor reviews and even worse box office.

"Nothing can possibly go wrong." (MGM/Photofest)

3

KILLING MACHINES: ROBOTS, CYBORGS, AND EVIL COMPUTERS

STANLEY STRANGELOVE

By the time *The Outer Limits* reached the airwaves in 1963, science fiction was all but dead at the neighborhood movie house. The golden age had passed, leaving little in its wake but the schlockiest of B movies riding the bottom of drive-in double bills. Of course, no movie genre ever really dies; it merely goes into hibernation. And when sci-fi returned to the big screen, it attained a respectability undreamed of in the days of *Earth vs. the Flying Saucers* and *The Beast with a Million Eyes*, primarily due to the efforts of one filmmaker.

Stanley Kubrick had already made a name for himself as a director by the early 1960s. His innovative, nonlinear heist picture *The Killing* had caught the attention of Kirk Douglas, with whom Kubrick made one of the great antiwar movies, *Paths of Glory*, as well as the big-budget spectacular *Spartacus*. After completing his controversial adaptation of Vladimir Nabokov's *Lolita*, Kubrick turned his attention to Peter George's best-selling novel *Red Alert*. His unconventional take on that book's nightmare nuclear-war scenario would become the first in a loose trilogy of science-fiction films directed by Kubrick, all of which revolved around a theme he would return to often: the uneasy relationship between humans and their technology.

Red Alert was a fairly straightforward Cold War thriller, similar to the novel *Fail-Safe* by Eugene Burdick and Harvey Wheeler, which was being adapted for the screen at about the same time by Sidney

Lumet. The story concerned an air force general in charge of a Strategic Air Command base who launches an unauthorized attack on the Soviet Union, nearly triggering World War III in the process. In the course of adapting the novel into a screenplay, the absurdity of the scenario kept foiling Kubrick's attempts to render it as a dramatic thriller. "The only way this thing really works for me is as a satire," he told producer James Harris, according to Vincent LoBrutto's *Stanley Kubrick: A Biography*. "My idea of doing it as a nightmare comedy came in the early weeks of working on the screenplay," he told interviewer Gene D. Phillips. "I found that in trying to put meat on the bones and to imagine the scenes fully, one had to keep leaving things out of it which were either absurd or paradoxical in order to keep it from being funny, and these things seem to be close to the heart of the scenes in question."

So why try to keep it from being funny? Why not hire Peter Sellers to play four different roles, so that a different version of the chameleonic comedian would be present at every pertinent location for the end of the world? (In the end, it didn't work out that way, as Sellers broke his leg before he could play B-52 commander Major Kong, a role that fortuitously went to Slim Pickens. Still, Sellers did end up playing the title character, as well as President Merkin Muffley and Group Captain Lionel Mandrake.) Kubrick brought in humorist Terry Southern (*The Magic Christian*) to punch up the screenplay of what came to be known as *Dr. Strangelove, or: How I Learned to Stop Worrying and Love the Bomb*.

To describe *Dr. Strangelove* as a science-fiction movie hardly seems adequate. It's a black comedy, a satire, and a farce that could pass stylistically for a conventional wartime documentary. If there's an intersection between *Why We Fight* and *Mad* magazine, you'll find *Dr. Strangelove* there. The film begins like no other comedy, with an ominous tracking shot through the "perpetually fog-shrouded wasteland below the Arctic peaks of the Zhokhov Islands," as a narrator speaks of ominous rumors about an ultimate weapon: a doomsday device. It's not exactly belly-busting stuff, but that's the method to Kubrick's madness. His film never looks like a conventional comedy, especially since he wisely excised a climactic pie fight from the final cut. He wants the laughs to catch in your throat. The opening-credits sequence, in which the bomber planes are refueled in midair, is pure documentary realism; it's only the accompanying music, "Try a Little Tenderness," that transforms it into a joke, and into a sexual metaphor that will carry on throughout the film. But for our purposes, the importance of this sequence is the way in which it reflects our desire to humanize or anthropomorphize our technology; it's a bookend to the closing shot of Pickens riding the nuke to Earth like a bucking bronco. Kubrick may have been suspicious of technology, but he was also seduced by it, and he recognized that these reactions were two sides of the same coin. After all, how could technology pose such a danger to us if we weren't so attracted to it in the first place?

Dr. Strangelove's doomsday machine, designed to be triggered automatically in case of attack and destroy all life on Earth, and programmed to resist any human attempt at disabling it, can certainly be seen as a precursor to *The Terminator*'s Skynet. But it was Kubrick's next film that would have the greatest effect on James Cameron. "As soon as I saw *2001: A Space Odyssey*, I knew I wanted to be a filmmaker," he told *Current Biography* magazine. "Until I saw that film, nothing in my life had ever lived up to my imagination . . . I just couldn't figure out how he did all that stuff. But I knew I just had to learn."

JOURNEY BEYOND THE STARS

Even before he had a story to tell, Kubrick knew he wanted to make a large-scale science-fiction epic in collaboration with one of the genre's top writers. That turned out to be Arthur C. Clarke, whose 1948 short story "The Sentinel" became the basis for the tentatively titled *Journey Beyond the Stars*. Over many months, Kubrick and Clarke hashed out a treatment, then worked simultaneously on the screenplay and a novel adaptation, both of which would come to be called *2001: A Space Odyssey*. Filming began in December 1965, with an eye toward releasing the movie in time for Christmas 1966. That didn't happen, as *2001* became the first of Kubrick's behemoth, long-delayed projects, with shooting continuing into 1967, followed by nearly a year's worth of special-effects work in post-production.

The film that emerged truly spanned the ages, from the "Dawn of Time" to "Beyond the Infinite." These segments are linked by a black monolith representing an alien intelligence present at each of man's evolutionary leaps. It is there when apes discover their first tool, a bone used to kill animals for food and establish dominance over rival tribes. It's a tool that looks as primitive to us today as a space station would appear to an advanced alien race, a point Kubrick makes with perhaps the most famous single edit of all time. The next monolith is discovered on the moon, and the third is found near Jupiter by Dave Bowman, the surviving member of a space mission that has gone haywire because the shipboard computer, HAL 9000, has gone insane. After disabling HAL and surviving a psychedelic light show and a dreamlike transformation in a Louis XVI–style hotel room, Bowman emerges as the next stage of human evolution, the Star Child. You know, your typical triumphant Hollywood ending.

When *2001* was finally released in April 1968, not everyone agreed it had been worth the wait. The New York premiere was disastrous, and the initial reviews were not kind; the old-guard critics regarded it as dull, plodding, and pretentious. Kubrick trimmed 19 minutes from the original 161-minute cut and found a much kinder reception as the film went into general release. *2001* struck a chord with the emerging counterculture, in part thanks to an advertising campaign selling the movie as "The Ultimate Trip." Despite its unconventional structure, minimal dialogue, and abstract finale, *2001* became an unlikely box-office sensation and cemented Kubrick's reputation as a master of cinema. It established the bold, baroque visual style, deliberate pacing, and meticulous attention to detail that would characterize all of his remaining films.

Many critics, even those who look favorably on *2001*, consider it a flaw that its human characters are so mundane and their dialogue so banal. In fact, what Kubrick is showing us here is that even the most exotic of wonders will eventually become run-of-the-mill through familiarity—even a trip to the moon. You'll see his point if you think about the last special-effects-laden blockbuster you saw in the theater. How mind-blowing would it have seemed twenty years ago? How ho-hum and forgettable does it look now? That's not true of *2001*, however. As James Cameron says on the film's special edition DVD release, "Even to this day, Kubrick's *2001: A Space Odyssey* remains the all-time great science fiction film." Its images are still so convincing that conspiracy theories persist that Kubrick faked the Apollo moon landings for NASA. In August of 2011, Samsung defended itself in a lawsuit brought by Apple on behalf of its iPad by claiming that Stanley Kubrick had actually invented the tablet computer . . . in *2001*.

In telling his cautionary tale about the perils of humans becoming too reliant on their technology, Kubrick embraced the latest in cutting-edge special effects, including front-screen projection and the slit-scan photography used to produce the climactic Star Gate sequence—a paradox that couldn't have been lost on an ironist like Kubrick. From a twenty-first-century perspective, it's almost as if his movie is itself a monolith, warning future filmmakers to resist allowing the coming advances in technology to overwhelm the human element of storytelling. If so, it's a warning that has gone largely unheeded.

CLOCKWORK VIOLENCE

The third film in Kubrick's loose trilogy of sci-fi cautionary tales about technology remains his most controversial work. In many ways, *A Clockwork Orange* is a tough movie to defend; the author of the book upon which it was based, Anthony Burgess, had serious misgivings about it, and even Kubrick seemed to have second thoughts when he withdrew it from distribution in Britain (allegedly due to copycat crimes, although the director never clarified his reasons). Its detractors find *A Clockwork Orange* morally reprehensible, or aesthetically didactic, or too weird, or too juvenile, or all of the above. It may be any or all of those things, but it's also an overpowering cinematic experience and one of the most successful attempts at conveying a subjective point of view in motion-picture history.

The Burgess novel, set in a near-future totalitarian Britain overrun by gang violence, was unreliably narrated by its central character, the young hoodlum Alex. Using an invented slang called *nadsat*, a blend of bastardized Russian and Cockney English, Alex tells the story of his ultra-violent youth, his capture by the authorities, and his participation in the experimental Ludovico treatment, by which he is reprogrammed into a law-abiding citizen incapable of acting on his criminal urges. Following a suicide attempt, and the attendant bad publicity for the government, Alex's free will is restored. In the final chapter, he outgrows his lawless ways and envisions a future as a family man.

Stanley Kubrick hadn't read that last chapter before adapting the Burgess novel for the screen, as it was omitted from American editions of the book. It's unlikely he'd have had much use for it anyway. What works on the page doesn't always translate to the screen (and whether the last chapter *does* work is certainly debatable—when Kubrick finally got around to reading it, he described it as "unconvincing and inconsistent with the style and intent of the book"), and the director already faced the daunting challenge of replicating Alex's unique point of view in cinematic terms. He accomplished this in two ways: He hired Malcolm McDowell, who delivered a wickedly charismatic performance as Alex, and he plugged the audience directly into the character's nervous system through his hyper-stylized technique. Kubrick's outsized imagery seems specifically designed to burrow deep into the viewer's subconscious, creating a stronger identification with a reprehensible character than would otherwise be possible. Critics who describe *A Clockwork Orange* as irresponsible, manipulative, and dangerous might well be describing Alex himself, because in this instance, movie and character can't be separated.

As a vision of the future, *Clockwork* couldn't be more different than *2001.* It's a sort of pop-art dystopia comprising a few sets (notably the Korova Milk Bar) and actual London-area locations chosen for their Brutalist architecture and general air of totalitarian rot. But it does share with both of its predecessors in Kubrick's unofficial trilogy a thematic concern with the perils of technology—in this case, the Ludovico technique that essentially transforms Alex into a mechanical man. Late in his life, Kubrick pursued a final project exploring the inverse theme—that of a mechanical boy yearning to be real. That film, *AI*, would eventually be made by Steven Spielberg following Kubrick's death in 1999. By then, the line between artificial intelligence and humanity had become increasingly blurred in the popular culture, as exemplified by the introduction of a kinder, gentler Terminator in *T2: Judgment Day*.

THE FINAL FRONTIER

Those who have never known a world without laptops, iPods, or Google may find this hard to believe, but for those of us who grew up before anyone had ever heard of Bill Gates or Steve Jobs, computers were futuristic creations we saw on *Star Trek*, along with phasers and transporter beams. You certainly couldn't fit one on your desktop; computers filled entire immense rooms, were covered with switches and blinking lights, and spat out reams of dot-matrix printouts to be pored over by only the most advanced intellects. And one thing was for certain: as soon as they got smart enough to realize how superior they were to the inferior organisms that created them, the computers would try to take over.

That's how it happened more than once on *Star Trek*, a series that was never above recycling a good idea during its original run (or in any of its many follow-ups, for that matter). In the second-season episode "The Changeling," the *Enterprise* encounters a space probe called *Nomad* that had been launched from Earth in the twenty-first century. It turns out that somewhere along its deep-space voyage of discovery, *Nomad* collided with a powerful alien probe and now operates on incomplete elements of both probes' programming. Due to this damage, *Nomad* mistakes Captain Kirk for its creator, Dr. Jackson Roykirk, but it also confuses its own orders with those of the alien probe. *Nomad* now believes its mission is to sterilize all imperfect biological organisms—that is, all human life.

Kirk defeats *Nomad* through a trope that has come to be known as the "logic bomb"; *Nomad* believes itself to be perfect, so when Kirk points out that the probe has mistaken its creator's identity, it can't deal with the contradiction. It overheats and keeps repeating "Error! Error! Error!"—a turn of events with which anyone who has held a data-entry job can identify. *Nomad* is confused long enough for the *Enterprise* crew to beam it into deep space, where it explodes from sheer cognitive dissonance. The immediate danger is over, but only a few episodes later, our heroes are forced to contend with "The Ultimate Computer."

The *Enterprise* is assigned to test the M5 multitronic unit, a new computer system capable of operating the ship without all that pesky human interference. Naturally, this doesn't sit well with Captain Kirk or the ever-crotchety Dr. McCoy, standing in for those members of the viewing audience living in fear of losing their jobs to automation. (Maybe this is reading too much into it, but the episode also plays as a commentary on William Shatner's notoriously out-of-control ego, with Kirk constantly bristling at the suggestion that he's no longer essential.) When the M5 begins shutting down power to unoccupied sections of the ship and diverting that energy to itself, Kirk grows concerned, but it's not until the computer fires on an unarmed vessel that the captain attempts to shut it down and regain control.

Unfortunately, unplugging the machine has no effect, as the M5 is now drawing power directly from the warp drive. The machine's creator, Dr. Daystrom, admits that he has programmed the computer with a sort of artificial intelligence based on his own mind, meaning that the M5 now thinks as he thinks. This is a bit of a problem, as it soon becomes evident that Daystrom is more than a little crazy. By now the M5 is firing on other Federation ships in the area, treating wargame simulations as actual combat and taking many lives in the process. Once again, Kirk is able to outwit a machine with his powers of confusion, this time by pointing out to the M5 that, in killing humans, it is contradicting its orders to protect them. The computer recognizes the error of its ways and assesses the death penalty on itself by shutting down.

GHOSTS IN THE MACHINE

A similar storyline powers the 1970 feature *Colossus: The Forbin Project*, based on a novel by Dennis Feltham Jones. Here the "ultimate computer" is designed by Dr. Charles Forbin (Eric Braeden), who has designed Colossus to take over the United States defense system, removing human error from the nuclear-war equation. As the president announces to the American people, Colossus will be "studying intelligence and data fed to it, and on the basis of those facts only deciding if an attack is about to be launched upon us." Located deep in the Rocky Mountains, Colossus is self-sufficient and impenetrable, has its own defenses, and controls all nuclear weapons. Nobody seems to have a problem with the fact that it has no off switch, not even an emergency presidential override button, but as Dr. Forbin assures everyone, the computer is not capable of original thought. Well . . .

Within minutes of being switched on, Colossus has detected its Russian counterpart, Guardian, the existence of which comes as a surprise to the president and his advisers. Colossus requests a link to Guardian, and soon the two machines are communicating in a mathematical language of their own devising. It dawns on Forbin that his creation is operating at a much higher level than he anticipated; when he attempts to cut off communication between the two supercomputers, Colossus and Guardian each launch missiles at targets in the United States and the USSR. Matters only escalate from there, with Colossus making more and more demands, eventually rendering Forbin a virtual prisoner in his own home under near-constant surveillance.

Thematically, *Colossus: The Forbin Project* is a fairly standard cautionary tale of man being usurped by his own technology, but as written by James Bridges (*The China Syndrome*, *Urban Cowboy*) and directed by Joseph Sargent (*White Lightning*, *The Taking of Pelham One Two Three*), it almost plays as a workplace comedy with higher stakes than usual. If *Mad Men* were to stay on the air long enough to reach the early '70s, it might look a bit like *Colossus*, which unfolds entirely in shades of beige, as chestnut-haired men in tan suits banter against a backdrop of mahogany wood paneling. At one point, Dr. Forbin shows Colossus how to make the perfect martini. It's that kind of movie, which means it's definitely a product of its time, but no less enjoyable for that.

By the early 1980s, the home computer had become a reality, although it was still a long way from the all-consuming apparatus we know today. Despite the lofty claims made for such early PCs as the TRS-80 and the Commodore PET, the first home systems were primarily used for primitive gaming, as any more ambitious aims would require computer-programming skills beyond the ability and patience of most consumers. So when *WarGames* was released in the summer of 1983, it was the right movie at the right time for more reasons than one.

Resembling a cross between *Colossus* and a John Hughes comedy, *WarGames* tapped into the Cold War paranoia of the Reagan era without ever lapsing into the hysterical jingoism of a *Red Dawn*. Its hero, David Lightman, is a direct cinematic ancestor of *The Social Network*'s Mark Zuckerberg, born just a few years too early to turn his mad hacking skillz into a billion-dollar company. It's not all bad, however, as Lightman is able to break into his high school's computer system and change his failing grade into a gentleman's C. (It would be another decade before most of us heard of the Internet, yet the notion of dialing into another computer via rotary phone still seemed plausible.) When Lightman attempts to dial into a computer game company in order to obtain bootleg copies of upcoming releases, he inadvertently hacks into NORAD's War Operations Plan Response system, or WOPR for short. So when he decides to play-test something called "Global Thermonuclear War," he gets a much more realistic experience than he bargained for: the WOPR begins to simulate an actual Soviet attack on America, pushing the superpowers closer to nuclear annihilation in the process.

The stakes may be high, but as directed by journeyman John Badham (*Blue Thunder*, *Short Circuit*), *WarGames* is about the breeziest doomsday thriller imaginable. The casting certainly helps, as Lightman, conceived as a dark loner by screenwriters Lawrence Lasker and Walter F. Parkes, becomes a much more likable and tech-savvy Ferris Bueller in the hands of Matthew Broderick. But even as Badham maintains a light touch on the proceedings, the suspense never flags, right up to the brink of DEFCON 1 (although the "logic bomb" finale, involving an analogy between nuclear war and tic-tac-toe, is perhaps a little too on-the-nose). The specific nuts-and-bolts technology may look incredibly dated now, but in portraying the increasing integration of computers into our day-to-day lives, *WarGames* was actually ahead of its time.

The same can't be said for Walt Disney's contemporary foray into cyber-entertainment, 1982's *TRON*. Like *WarGames*, *TRON* features a charming young lead actor portraying a videogame enthusiast and proto-hacker, in this case Jeff Bridges as Flynn. But unlike *WarGames*, *TRON* dares to visualize the world inside its computers, a feat that entails dressing its cast in luminescent leotards and dropping them into a black-light poster.

Flynn is a former programmer for software company ENCOM, who struck out on his own after co-worker Ed Dillinger (David Warner) stole some of his best games and passed them off as his own, earning a promotion to CEO in the process. Flynn has been trying to find evidence of Dillinger's wrongdoing using a hacking program called Clu (also played by Bridges, as most of the actors in the film do double duty as real-world humans and personifications of the programs they've created). During one of his searches, Flynn accidentally sets off an experimental laser that digitizes him and transports him into what we now call cyberspace. Once inside the computer world, Flynn is forced to compete in videogame duels at the behest of the Master Control Program, the artificial intelligence that rules cyberspace. Flynn teams up with a program called Tron (Bruce Boxleitner) to overthrow the MCP and free the digital world from enslavement.

If you've never seen *TRON*, this may all sound a little silly, but rest assured, it's even goofier than you imagine. Give it credit for one thing, though: it's the only movie that looks like *TRON*. Widely touted at the time of its release as being the first film to make extensive use of computer graphics, *TRON* is actually much more reliant on traditional animation and special effects than on cutting-edge technology. The computer-world scenes were shot in black and white on an empty soundstage, then made to look digital through handmade methods in post-production. Several hundred animators were employed to add the light effects to the actors' costumes, after which this footage was combined with digitally animated backgrounds. (In all, about fifteen minutes of *TRON* consists of computer animation, a tremendous achievement for the time.) The result is a cockeyed kaleidoscope of geometric shapes, neon colors, and weirdly disembodied actors that could have happened only in the early '80s. Of course, that didn't stop Disney from returning to the well nearly thirty years later for the much-belated sequel *TRON: Legacy*. An oddly self-serious attempt at mining what was essentially a kiddie matinee for a labyrinthine, *Matrix*-like mythology, the latter film did succeed in demonstrating how far computer imaging had advanced since its predecessor by digitally reincarnating the youthful Jeff Bridges. Despite its strong performance at the box office, however, it was a singularly joyless misfire.

WESTWORLD AND BEYOND

Computers may become self-aware, they may be able to voice original thoughts in neutral yet subtly condescending tones, and they may even have the capability to launch every nuclear weapon on the planet. But no matter how much artificial intelligence they're able to develop, they'll always be completely useless in a barroom brawl. That's where the robots come in.

As we've already seen, humanoid-looking robots date back at least as far as Fritz Lang's *Metropolis* in 1927. Harlan Ellison would tell you he created the Terminator's inspiration in his *Outer Limits* episode "Demon with a Glass Hand," starring Robert Culp as an android from the future. But if anyone can claim to be the Terminator's spiritual godfather, it would have to be the late techno-thriller author and occasional filmmaker Michael Crichton, who wrote and directed *Westworld* in 1973.

Inspired by a visit to Disneyland's Hall of Presidents, Crichton envisioned a technologically advanced theme park where the attractions go haywire. (He would later revisit this idea on a grander scale in *Jurassic Park*.) Rather than have patrons terrorized by pistol-packing Abe Lincolns and Millard Fillmores, Crichton populated his Delos resort with androids programmed to allow visitors to live out their wildest fantasies, whether in the Roman Empire, medieval times, or the wild west. Richard Benjamin stars as a first-time visitor to the park trying to shrug off his wimpy, citified persona for a few days by playing outlaw in an Old West setting. He gets more than he bargained for when the ostensibly harmless robots begin malfunctioning due to an electronic infection—in other words, the world's first computer virus.

Yul Brynner pays homage to his role in *The Magnificent Seven* as The Gunslinger, a black-hatted foil for the Westworld patrons that becomes an unstoppable killing machine once its circuitry gets scrambled. Brynner's methodical, unrelenting pursuit of Benjamin, as well as The Gunslinger's crude digital "robot's-eye view" shots, undoubtedly influenced James Cameron, although the director also saw an opportunity to improve on what Crichton had achieved. "We'd had things like *Westworld*, where Yul Brynner's face falls off and there's a transistor radio underneath," Cameron told *Film Comment*. He found this unsatisfying because "you don't feel that this mechanism could have been inside moving those facial features. So it started from the idea of doing this sort of definitive movie robot, what I've always wanted to see."

Brynner's effectively menacing Gunslinger may not have been definitive, but it struck enough of a chord with movie audiences to make *Westworld* a modest box-office success. In retrospect, it's more of a fun concept than a fully realized film—it really does play like a rough draft for *Jurassic Park*—but it looks like a masterpiece compared to its 1976 sequel *Futureworld*, which was produced without Crichton's involvement. (Brynner contributes a brief cameo, reprising The Gunslinger in a dream sequence.) A CBS television series, *Beyond Westworld*, followed in 1980 but was canceled after only three episodes.

It appeared that history was destined to warp in on itself in 2002 when *Variety* reported that Arnold Schwarzenegger had signed to produce and star in a remake of *Westworld* for Warner Bros. "Schwarzenegger is poised to reprise the Yul Brynner [role] in *Westworld* of a robotic Old West gunman programmed to be slain by wannabe gunslinger tourists in a fantasy vacation," wrote

Michael Fleming. "When the robot's circuits go awry, he becomes a real killing machine and hunts the visitors." The piece makes no mention of the role's resemblance to Schwarzenegger's star-making vehicle, although the Austrian Oak is quoted as saying, "I loved the original film when I saw it in 1973 and have wanted to remake it for several years." Given that the same article trumpeted Arnold's plan to return as Conan the Barbarian, a role that has since passed him by, it's probably safe to assume that a real-life Westworld will open before a Schwarzenegger-headlined remake ever sees the light of day.

Of course, if a real-life Westworld *did* open tomorrow, it's a sure bet that the most lucrative attraction would be the brothels stocked with lifelike sex robots. Just as pornography paved the way for the commercialization of the Internet, rest assured that the sex industry is on the cutting edge of humanoid robot development. According to a 2010 CNN report, "the world's most sophisticated talking female sex robot," Roxxxy, can be yours for a mere $7,000. As always, however, reality is lagging behind Hollywood, as Roxxxy's creator Douglas Hines admits, "She doesn't vacuum or cook." That being the case, the 1975 satirical thriller *The Stepford Wives* is still ahead of its time.

Based on the 1972 novel by Ira Levin (*Rosemary's Baby*), *Stepford* stars Katharine Ross as Joanna Eberhart, an aspiring photographer and mother of two who reluctantly leaves her vibrant New York City lifestyle behind when her husband, Walter (Peter Masterson), pushes for a move to the suburbs. Stepford Village is a quaint white-picket-fence community straight out of a storybook, right down to the cheerful neighbor lady greeting the new family with a casserole. But it soon becomes apparent to Joanna that there's something wrong with the women of Stepford; they all wear near-identical floor-length dresses, their conversations all seem to come straight out of Madison Avenue ("I'll just die if I don't get that recipe!"), and they're all way too devoted to their lumpy, middle-aged husbands, particularly in the bedroom.

As scripted by William Goldman, *Stepford* is a satire of suburban conformity and a tech-savvy update on *Invasion of the Body Snatchers*.

The women of Stepford aren't being replaced by pod people, but by robots built by creepy white men of privilege who can't deal with the changes being brought about by the women's liberation movement. (And, as with *Westworld*, Disneyland is the inspiration, as one of the Stepford men is a former Imagineer for the park.) Unfortunately, *Stepford* is one of those movies that's more fun in theory than in execution; the audience is so far ahead of the characters that the picture drags for long stretches, livened up only by a saucy Paula Prentiss as Joanna's wised-up neighbor. Still, the original *Stepford Wives* builds to an appropriately sinister conclusion, something that can't be said for the wildly incoherent 2004 remake directed by Frank Oz. Tacking on one ludicrous false ending after another, this box-office disaster once again demonstrates the pitfalls of modern Hollywood's "more is more" approach when it comes to revitalizing tried-and-true material. As we'll see, not even *The Terminator* is immune to the perils of excess.

KILLING MACHINES: FIVE HONORABLE MENTIONS

***Alphaville* (1965)**—You could make the argument that Jean-Luc Godard (*Breathless*, *Weekend*) was the first to fuse science-fiction concepts with film noir style, decades before *The Terminator* and *Blade Runner*. Of course, Godard being Godard, it's never that straightforward. Eddie Constantine, who had played detective Lemmy Caution in a series of French films, reinvents the role here as a world-weary private eye in a dystopian future where forbidden words disappear, citizens showing emotion are executed, and everything is overseen by a sentient computer called Alpha 60 (disturbingly voiced by a throat-cancer patient using an electronic voicebox). As with much of Godard's French New Wave work, *Alphaville* favors abstraction over linear narrative, and alienating techniques (inappropriately brassy musical cues over mundane scenes) and absurdist humor (a pair of scientists named Dr. Heckell and Dr. Jeckell) over traditional suspense. Godard does employ at least one tried-and-true sci-fi cliché, as Caution defeats the Alpha 60 by posing a riddle it cannot solve. Captain Kirk would be proud.

***THX-1138* (1971)**—In his best-known work, George Lucas created the much-beloved Laurel-and-Hardy robot duo of R2D2 and C3PO. But in his slightly less popular debut feature, an expanded version of his USC student film, Lucas unleashed a decidedly unlovable robot police force on a conformist society of the future. Cerebral and visually striking in a minimalist style light-years removed from his overstuffed space operas, *THX 1138* is certainly no crowd-pleaser, but despite its narrative shortcomings it exerts a certain hypnotic fascination.

***Doctor Who: Genesis of the Daleks* (1975)**—A staple of British television for nearly fifty years, the time-traveling, ever-evolving Doctor has faced his share of evil machines over the decades, none more popular than the Daleks. These overgrown fire hydrants with their deadly rayguns and unnerving electronic shrieks of "Exterminate!" have been staples of the *Doctor Who* series since the early '60s, but this six-part episode starring Tom Baker as the iconic Fourth Doctor may be their most popular appearance of all. In a sort of reverse-*Terminator* scenario, the Doctor travels back in time in hopes of stopping the Daleks from ever being created, thus preventing their eons-long reign of terror. It's an entertaining variation on the old "Would you kill Hitler as a child?" conundrum, presented with the series' usual mix of cheeky humor, Velveeta special effects, and sweeping sense of adventure.

***The Hitchhiker's Guide to the Galaxy* (1978)**—In this irresistible satire of all things science fictional, which began as a six-part BBC Radio series, Douglas Adams explores the banality of evil through the products of the Sirius Cybernetics Corporation. These useless technological achievements include argumentative elevators, obnoxiously cheerful shipboard computers, and a drink dispenser that produces only a liquid that is "almost, but not quite, entirely unlike tea," but their most famous creation is undoubtedly Marvin the Paranoid Android, a relentlessly depressing robot. Marvin may not be as deadly as a Terminator, but he's arguably worse company.

***Bill & Ted's Bogus Journey* (1991)**—Bill S. Preston, Esq., and Ted "Theodore" Logan (Alex Winter and Keanu Reeves) face many perils in the sequel to their *Excellent Adventure*, including the devil, the Easter Bunny, and a death-defying game of Twister with the Grim Reaper. Most perilous of all are the "evil robot us-es" sent from the future to kill Bill and Ted, disrupt the Battle of the Bands, and prevent the dude-topian world of tomorrow from ever happening. It's fun to watch Winter and Reeves put a mischievous spin on their sweet-natured doofus characters, but righteousness prevails in the end when two "good robot us-es" created by hairy, large-rumped alien Station intervene. They don't make sequels like this anymore.

THE SIX MILLION DOLLAR MAN

One of the few pop-culture artifacts of the 1970s that managed to stay buried until very recently, *The Six Million Dollar Man* began as a ninety-minute movie for television based on the novel *Cyborg* by former air force pilot Martin Caidin. First airing on March 7, 1973, on ABC, the TV movie starring Lee Majors was a reasonably faithful adaptation of Caidin's story, summed up neatly in the narration that would open every subsequent episode: "Steve Austin, astronaut, a man barely alive. Gentlemen, we can rebuild him. We have the technology. We have the capability to make the world's first bionic man. Better than he was before. Better, stronger, faster."

Based on the TV movie's encouraging ratings, ABC ordered two more ninety-minute specials: "Wine, Women and War" and "Solid Gold Kidnapping." As produced by *Battlestar Galactica* creator Glen A. Larson, these movies of the week were an attempt at establishing Steve Austin as a suave 007-style superspy, a development that didn't sit well with either Caidin or the TV audience. Enter new producer Harve Bennett, who reshaped the series around his star's laconic Marlboro Man persona. The weekly, one-hour version of *The Six Million Dollar Man* was launched in January 1974 and immediately shot into the top ten of the Nielsen ratings.

The series was no model of sophisticated storytelling, and Lee Majors was never going to be mistaken for De Niro, but his affable, down-to-earth qualities helped *The Six Million Dollar Man* keep one foot grounded in reality, no matter how far it wandered into its own little zone of weirdness. Finding suitably formidable adversaries for their hero proved to be a challenge for the producers, but that challenge resulted in some of the series' most enjoyable episodes. It was not enough for Steve Austin to do battle with Bigfoot—it had to be a bionic Bigfoot assembled by aliens from another galaxy. And then there were the robots.

The first-season episode "Day of the Robot" introduced the next logical step beyond a bionic human—a fully functioning robot duplicate of Austin's scientist friend, played by John Saxon. Of course, the machine proves to be no match for the bionic man, but its creator escapes, only to resurface in the appropriately titled "Return of the Robot Maker." This time it is Austin's boss, the plaid-jacketed Oscar Goldman (Richard Anderson), who is replaced by a duplicate, but in the end Austin is able to tell the genuine article from the fake because "robots don't sweat." The real fun began on the spinoff series *The Bionic Woman*, which introduced a line of "fembots" manufactured by a scenery-chewing John Houseman. (Has there ever been a more tantalizing TV episode title than "Fembots in Las Vegas"?) Also on *The Bionic Woman*, Steve's female bionic counterpart Jaime Sommers (Lindsay Wagner) took on a supercomputer named Alex, programmed to set off the world's nuclear arsenal, in the two-part "Doomsday Is Tomorrow," a low-rent *Dr. Strangelove Meets Colossus: The Forbin Project*.

Neither *The Six Million Dollar Man* nor *The Bionic Woman* could survive the '70s, although several reunion movies later aired. In 2007 NBC launched a short-lived "re-imagining" of *Bionic Woman*, but it failed to connect with an audience. In December 2011, the first season of *The Six Million Dollar Man* was finally released on DVD, in hopes of inspiring a new generation of bionic enthusiasts to run through their backyards in slow motion.

Charlton Heston in *Planet of the Apes*: "I can't help thinking that somewhere in the universe there has to be something better than man."
(20th Century-Fox/Photofest)

4

NO FATE BUT WHAT WE MAKE: TIME TRAVEL

THE FOURTH DIMENSION

Reasonable people can disagree about the first appearance of time travel in literature. Was Ebenezer Scrooge traveling through time in *A Christmas Carol*, or merely dreaming? Did Mark Twain's Connecticut Yankee actually find himself in King Arthur's court, or was it just a hallucination brought on by a blow to the head? Your mileage may vary, but few would dispute that the first time machine was invented by H. G. Wells (in a literary sense, not a literal one, despite what you may have seen in the movie *Time After Time*). In fact, Wells' creation of the science-fiction staple predates his 1895 novel *The Time Machine* by seven years, as it first appears in his short story "The Chronic Argonauts."

It's only fitting, then, that cinema's first time machine appeared in an adaptation of the Wells novel, directed by George Pal, one of the giants of the '50s golden age. In fact, the Wells estate was so impressed with Pal's version of *War of the Worlds*, they allowed him to option any of the author's other science-fiction works. Pal chose *The Time Machine*, a socialist allegory in which Wells speculated about a future division of the haves and have-nots into two different species, the Eloi and the Morlocks. Pal and screenwriter David Duncan ditched the political angle but for the most part stuck closely to the Wells story.

Pal's film opens in Victorian London, on New Year's Eve, 1899, at the home of an eccentric inventor played by Rod Taylor. The inventor has assembled a group of friends to witness a demonstration; using what appears to be a delicate piece of dollhouse furniture, he will prove that fourth-dimensional travel is possible. When the little gizmo disappears, his colleagues are less than impressed by what they reckon to be a cheap parlor trick. But after they leave, Taylor retreats to cellar to perform a full-scale version of the experiment, with himself in the driver's seat of the time machine.

This kicks off the cleverest and most purely enjoyable stretch of the film, as Taylor slowly makes his way through the years, with the passage of time marked by time-lapse photography, stop-motion animation, and the changing fashions on the department store mannequin visible through the basement window. Candles quickly burn down, shadows skip across the ceiling, and a snail speeds his way across the floor. The time machine itself is a marvelous, period-appropriate design built out of a Victorian barber chair, brass rails, hand levers, and a spinning wheel at the back. (Pal's prop became a cult object over the years; it was sold at auction in 1971 and later turned up in a thrift store, where it was purchased by collector Bob Burns. It can be glimpsed in the background of a convention scene in 1984's *Gremlins*.)

Departing from the Wells novel, the time machine makes several stops throughout the twentieth century. Taylor witnesses World Wars I, II, and III, the third taking place in 1966 and constituting the least convincing sequence in the film, as London is destroyed in miniature by a volcano spouting lava made from red-dyed oatmeal. It looks more like a fourth-grade science experiment than a major motion picture's special-effects centerpiece, but Taylor is soon on his way again, this time into the far distant future portrayed in the novel. But while the film retains the split Eloi and Morlock societies from Wells, the intended social commentary of this division is largely absent. The Eloi resemble a commune of weirdly detached flower children; had *Time Machine* been made a few years later, their appearance and behavior could easily be taken for a satire of hippie culture, but for 1960, that's a bit of a reach. The Morlocks are simply cannibalistic underworld mutants, remnants of those who took to underground bomb shelters to survive the nuclear holocaust, too easily destroyed by fire in the film's hasty climax.

Despite its flaws, however, *The Time Machine* is a generally charming cinematic introduction to the concept of time travel.

The time travel films that followed in the early '60s tended to follow the same basic template drawn from the Wells novel. The AIP cheapie *Beyond the Time Barrier* appeared in theaters at around the same time as *The Time Machine* in order to capitalize on the publicity for the bigger attraction. Directed by Edgar G. Ulmer (*The Black Cat*, *Detour*), this extremely low-budget effort concerns an air force pilot who flies through a wormhole and finds himself in a post-apocalyptic future populated, in familiar fashion, by warring races of humans and mutants. In 1964's *The Time Travelers*, scientists who have developed a viewscreen upon which they can observe the future find that the screen is actually a portal through which they can enter the year 2071, where once again humans and mutants battle in a world decimated by nuclear war.

It's safe to say movies weren't exactly exploring all the creative possibilities offered by time travel, but by the mid-'60s, several television shows began to deal with the tropes and temporal paradoxes we've come to know and love. The fall of 1966 saw the debut of not only *Star Trek*, which would deal with time travel in a number of episodes, including the Harlan Ellison–penned "City on the Edge of Forever," but *The Time Tunnel*, an ambitious and very expensive series produced by master of disaster Irwin Allen. (Let the record show that the Sherwood Schwartz–created sitcom *It's About Time*, which was essentially *Gilligan's Island* with cavemen and dinosaurs, also debuted the same week as *Star Trek* and *The Time Tunnel*. An embarrassment of riches, to be sure.)

The pilot episode of *The Time Tunnel*, which cost a then-whopping $500,000 to produce, posits a costly government program called Project Tic-Toc operating in a secret facility 800 stories beneath the Arizona desert. In the episode's most realistic touch, a crotchety U.S. senator has flown in to inspect the site, grumble about the waste of taxpayer dollars, and pull the plug on the operation unless he sees immediate results. Impetuous young scientist James Darren dashes into the massive time tunnel and is transported back to the deck of the *Titanic* on the eve of its destruction. (This is an aspect of time travel we'll see play out over and over again. No one is ever transported back to a random Dairy Queen on a Tuesday in 1957. If you're sent back in time, you're almost certain to arrive at a historically significant event.) Subsequent episodes would follow the same formula, transporting Darren and co-star Robert Colbert to the Old West, Pearl Harbor, and other destinations easily re-created on studio backlots and augmented by appropriate feature-film footage.

When the time-travel concept returned to the big screen in 1968, the same year as Kubrick's *2001*, audiences around the world would be captivated by a dark future in which humanity is dominated not by machines, but by apes.

PLANET OF THE APES

In 1963, French novelist Pierre Boulle published *La Planète des Singes*, which roughly translated into English as *Monkey Planet*. Boulle considered it a minor work, with little potential for successful translation to the motion-picture screen, unlike his earlier book *The Bridge Over the River Kwai*. American producer Arthur P. Jacobs disagreed and optioned the rights to the novel, which told the story of a human astronaut who found himself on a planet where apes were the dominant species. At first, it appeared Boulle's estimation of his own work was correct, as Jacobs had trouble convincing any studio that the story could be brought to the screen without audiences laughing derisively at actors in gorilla suits. Jacobs decided he needed a Hollywood star on his side to help convince a studio of the project's marketability, and after approaching the likes of Marlon Brando and Burt Lancaster, he finally convinced Charlton Heston to come aboard. Heston in turn lured his friend Franklin Schaffner, who had directed him in *The War Lord*, to sign on for *Planet of the Apes*. *Twilight Zone* creator Rod Serling was commissioned to write the script and, after thirty drafts, finally turned in a workable screenplay.

Twentieth Century Fox president Richard Zanuck was intrigued by the project but unconvinced that the apes could be made to look realistic enough to pull an audience into the drama. He commissioned a makeup test, offering the princely sum of $5,000 for Jacobs and company to convince him it could be done. With the help of actors Edward G. Robinson (who played the orangutan Dr. Zaius in the test), James Brolin (made up as a chimp), and Heston, a brief scene was shot using crude makeup designs by Fox stalwart Ben Nye. It was enough to convince Zanuck, but Serling's script was still an obstacle. Like Boulle's novel, it depicted a technologically advanced ape society, complete with planes, helicopters, and an ultra-modern city of apes. It was a budget-buster, but with the help of screenwriter Michael Wilson, who overhauled Serling's script, Schaffner downgraded ape society to a more primitive, and affordable, level.

By the time shooting started on May 21, 1967, the aging and frail Robinson had bowed out of the role of Zaius, on the grounds that daily application of the orangutan makeup would prove too taxing. Shakespearian actor Maurice Evans took the role instead, while Roddy McDowall and Kim Hunter agreed to be transformed into the chimps Cornelius and Zira. For McDowall in particular, it would prove to be a career-defining decision.

As the film opens, Heston's astronaut Taylor is aboard a spaceship with several crew members in suspended animation, en route to the distant star Alpha Centauri. Taylor has no qualms about never seeing his home planet Earth again, and no regrets that the faster-than-light travel of his spacecraft has accelerated him through time, meaning that everyone he ever knew is long since dead. Somewhere out there, he reasons, there has to be something better than man. When the ship crashes on an unknown planet, Taylor and the two surviving members of his crew make their way through a desert wasteland in hopes of finding life before they expire.

This opening half hour of *Planet of the Apes* is perhaps the least likely launching pad imaginable for a successful Hollywood film franchise. For a long stretch of screen time, we are simply watching three characters traveling slowly across a blighted landscape, accompanied by Jerry Goldsmith's eerie, tribal score. Heston's Taylor character is so caustic and embittered, so sarcastically dismissive of every attempt his colleagues make at suggesting a hopeful outcome, we might well be watching a Beckett play. Eventually the astronauts come across some vegetation, then a freshwater spring guarded by a ring of scarecrows. Their clothes are stolen while they're swimming, and when they pursue the thieves into a cornfield, the film unleashes its most effectively terrifying sequence. The thieves are revealed to be mute humans, barely evolved beyond cavemen. They panic at the sound of approaching horses and begin to scatter. When the horses arrive, the camera zooms in on one of the riders to reveal an armed gorilla soldier.

Taylor is shot in the throat, captured, and brought to a city of apes ruled by a council of orangutans, with chimpanzees as scientists and gorillas as the military. At this point, the tone of the film shifts to social satire, as Taylor is studied, poked, prodded, and tortured before finally revealing his ability to speak, with perhaps the movie's most quoted line, "Take your stinkin' paws off me, you damn dirty ape!" At this point he is brought up on charges and forced to defend himself before a tribunal of three orangutans, with the assistance of sympathetic chimp scientists Cornelius and Zira. This middle section of *Planet of the Apes* has been interpreted as anything from an animal-rights polemic to a powerful statement on race relations in America to a veiled commentary on the HUAC era, but it probably shouldn't be taken *too* seriously; Schaffner tips his hand with a visual joke in which the orangutan tribunal reenacts the famous three-wise-monkeys pose of "see no evil, hear no evil, speak no evil."

In the final act, Cornelius and Zira help Taylor and his assigned mate Nova (Linda Harrison) escape to the Forbidden Zone, where they find evidence of an advanced human civilization predating the ape society. This leads into the shocker of a final image, much parodied since but undeniably powerful at the time, in which Taylor discovers the remains of the Statue of Liberty on the beach and realizes he has been on Earth all along. (Naturally, that ending survived from the early script penned by twist-master Rod Serling.)

While undeniably a product of its time (as are all the *Apes* films), the original *Planet of the Apes* retains the same fascination it held for audiences when it debuted on February 8, 1968. The simple yet effective role reversal of its premise, the makeup effects and the ability of the actors to convey strong characterizations from beneath layers of latex, Charlton Heston's antihero performance—showy, but uncompromising toward any notion of "likability"—and that mind-melter of an ending all added up to an unexpected monster hit for Fox. At that time, sequels were far from automatic for even the biggest box-office performers, and in any case, *Planet* seemed self-contained and closed off from any possibility of continuation. Nonetheless, the people demanded more apes, and Richard Zanuck was determined to give the people what they wanted.

One person who wasn't enthused about the idea was Charlton Heston, who told Zanuck, "I don't want to do a sequel. That's like the Andy Hardy series." Still, Heston realized that the original *Apes* would never have been made without Zanuck's support, so he agreed to do it on the condition that his character be killed off in the first scene. (A compromise was reached in which Taylor disappeared early in the picture, only to return and die at the end.) Both Rod Serling and Pierre Boulle submitted story ideas (Boulle's *Planet of the Men* script involved Taylor and Nova discovering a lost civilization of humans in the jungle and leading an uprising against the apes), but in the end, it was British poet and screenwriter Paul Dehn who would author what came to be known as *Beneath the Planet of the Apes*. Dehn would go on to become the guiding creative force for the rest of the *Apes* series, and thus a major influence on the Terminator franchise.

Dehn was obsessed with apocalyptic themes and the looming specter of nuclear annihilation, and his story for the sequel reflected those preoccupations. Whether consciously or not, Dehn's script echoed the original time-travel story, H. G. Wells' *The Time Machine*, as once again a man from our era travels into the far distant future to find mankind split between surface dwellers and underground mutants. (Of course, Wells didn't think of the talking monkeys, so he couldn't have been *that* much of a genius.) Here the traveler is Brent (James Franciscus), an astronaut from Taylor's time sent on a rescue mission to find the spaceship and crew from the first movie. Instead, he finds not only a city of apes, but the mutants of the

Forbidden Zone, who worship an atomic bomb with the power to destroy the planet.

Like its predecessor and the rest of the *Apes* movies, *Beneath* offered a cracked reflection of the turbulent late '60s and early '70s, in this case commenting on the then-raging Vietnam War, as the imperialist gorilla army launches an unprovoked attack on the underworld dwellers, while young hippie chimps protest. But although *Beneath* exerts a certain bizarre fascination, it doesn't really hold together. Franciscus appears to have been cast primarily for his resemblance to Heston, an illusion that shatters when the two actors finally share the same frame and Franciscus looks more like Heston's Mini-Me. McDowall, off directing a film in Scotland, is absent altogether, so David Watson fills in as Cornelius. The lower budget resulted in less impressive special effects, and while the matte paintings serving as the ruins of New York have a creaky old-school charm, the use of ape masks rather than full makeups in the crowd scenes is extremely noticeable. The nihilistic finale, in which a dying Taylor chooses to set off the doomsday device rather than allow either of these mad civilizations to continue, could have been powerful, but it's so abrupt and clumsily staged, it's only laughable.

But even the destruction of the planet wasn't enough to put a halt to the *Apes* franchise once *Beneath* proved to be a box-office hit in its own right. Producer Arthur Jacobs sent a telegram to Dehn reading, "Apes exist. Sequel required," putting the pressure on the screenwriter to figure out a way to continue the story. His solution was ingenious, and the resulting *Escape from the Planet of Apes* is the point at which the series really becomes interesting from a time-travel perspective.

As the film opens, an American spacecraft has splashed down in the Pacific Ocean, where it is retrieved by a military contingent. When three astronauts emerge from the ship and remove their helmets, they are revealed to be . . . ape-onauts! Specifically, they are Cornelius (once again played by McDowall, making a welcome return from his one-picture hiatus), Zira (Hunter), and another chimp scientist, Dr. Milo (Sal Mineo). As it turns out, the chimps had salvaged Taylor's spaceship, and the brilliant Milo figured out how to get it working again, so that they were able to escape the Earth just in time to witness its destruction from space. Passing back through the same time wormhole that originally sent Taylor into the future, they have now arrived in Earth's past, specifically 1973. With this clever turn of events, Dehn not only built a detour around the dead end he'd constructed in *Beneath*, but opened up a whole new superhighway of satirical possibilities, as *Escape* essentially plays out as a reversal of the original film. Now our sympathies shift to the apes, who are at first caged and studied, then interrogated before a presidential commission, then fêted by swinging '70s high society in scenes that suggest Tom Wolfe's *Radical Chic* with talking chimps in place of Black Panthers. (Not such an off-the-wall notion, as we'll soon see.)

While the first hour or so of *Escape* generally plays as comedy, the film takes on a darker tone when the president's science adviser Dr. Hasslein (Eric Braeden of *Colossus: The Forbin Project*) recommends killing the chimps in hopes of changing the course of history and preventing apes from becoming Earth's dominant species. Complicating matters is the fact that Zira has recently given birth. With the help of friendly circus owner Armando (Ricardo Montalbán), Cornelius, Zira, and their baby chimp go into hiding. Eventually they are tracked down and killed, but this time Dehn left himself a back door in case more sequels were ordered: the baby chimp has survived, and he can talk.

Dehn's instincts proved sound, as a fourth *Apes* film was soon commissioned—one that would go on to become the most controversial entry in the series. *Conquest of the Planet of the Apes* opens in 1991, eight years after a plague has killed every dog and cat on Earth. Missing their pets, humans began to adopt apes, who eventually became servants, and now essentially slaves. The baby chimp from *Escape* has grown up to become Caesar, who bears a remarkable resemblance to his father, as he is also played by Roddy McDowall. Forced to go into hiding among his fellow apes, Caesar is exposed to the cruel treatment and brutal training regimen of Ape Management. When his friend Armando is killed trying to protect Caesar's secret, the talking chimp organizes a violent ape rebellion against the human oppressors.

Each *Apes* sequel had seen its budget slashed compared to its predecessor, and *Conquest* was no exception. Director J. Lee Thompson (*Cape Fear*, *The Guns of Navarone*) made the most of the limitations, shooting much of the film against the Brutalist backdrop of the University of California at Irvine campus and employing a handheld camera and wide-angle lenses to freaky, disorienting effect. McDowall proved up to the challenge of conveying a darker chimp character. His fiery final speech, in which he heralds "the inevitable day of man's downfall," when human cities lie buried in radioactive rubble, is the actor's finest moment in the series.

The original cut of *Conquest* was far more violent than its predecessors. The ape rebellion was modeled after the Watts riots of 1965, and the story's parallels to the civil-rights struggle and the Black Power movement were hard to miss. Fearing the loss of the family audience that had buoyed the box-office grosses of the earlier installments, Fox ordered the violence trimmed and brought in McDowall to record a more hopeful coda to his revolutionary rhetoric. The reworked ending blunted the movie's impact (although the restored original cut is now available as part of the Blu-ray boxed set of all five *Apes* films), but it may have unwittingly provided a solution to a narrative conundrum Dehn had created.

With the first four *Apes* films, Dehn felt he had crafted a circular timeline—but he'd really created a temporal paradox. After all, how could Caesar have led the revolution that resulted in the future domination of Earth by apes if his parents were time-traveling apes from that future Earth? Cornelius and Zira would never have existed without Caesar's efforts in the past, but Caesar could never have existed without Cornelius and Zira. It's an endless loop of confusion, and a perfect example of what makes time travel such a fun, yet problematic, subject for contemplation. Some may argue that time is a closed loop, while others insist that any changes to the past will result in the creation of alternate timeline, and nobody can ever be proven right or wrong due to the inconvenient fact that time travel doesn't exist.

The fifth and final film of the original series, *Battle for the Planet of the Apes*, suggests the possibility that, to put it in *Terminator* terms, "the future is not set" and "there's no fate but what we make." Paul Dehn had planned an even darker final chapter than *Conquest*, with Caesar as a mad emperor conducting experiments on humans to remove their power of speech, but Fox and producer Arthur Jacobs were determined to end the series on a family-friendly note. The husband-and-wife screenwriting team of John and Joyce Corrington was brought in to pick up the story of Caesar a decade or so after the events of *Conquest*. The prophesied nuclear war has come to pass, and now Caesar and the surviving apes live in a primitive tree-house community that will presumably one day become Ape City. Humans live among the apes, not as slaves, but not as equals, either. Those who remained in the city when the bombs fell and survived have become underground mutants—forebears of those seen in *Beneath the Planet of the Apes*.

On an expedition to the Forbidden Zone, Caesar views tapes of his parents and learns the secret of Earth's future destruction. The fragile peace between ape and human is threatened by a gorilla mutiny sparked by General Aldo (Claude Akins) and by an attack on Ape City by the mutants of the Forbidden Zone. The ensuing combat scenes proved too ambitious for the limited budget, and as a result, *Battle* is probably the least compelling of the original *Apes* films. (It's also a bit ridiculous that the apes have evolved seemingly overnight from the mute slaves of the previous film.) It does have its points of interest, though, notably the suggestion that the bleak future seen in the first two films might be averted, with Paul Dehn's circular time loop broken. The movie ends on an ambiguous note, with the possibility but not the promise that ape and man might find lasting peace as equals. The idea that a future foreseen may not be inevitable, after all, would play out again in the *Terminator* franchise, with a rather different outcome.

THE 1980S GO BACK TO THE FUTURE

It was morning in America, and time travel was booming. For whatever reason, the early to mid-1980s were a peak period for the genre, as a number of time-hopping films reached theaters in addition to *The Terminator*. The cycle actually kicked off in 1979, with a movie that revisited H. G. Wells' original *Time Machine* from a fresh perspective. Written and directed by Nicholas Meyer (*Star Trek II: The Wrath of Khan*), *Time After Time* asserts that Wells himself actually invented a working time machine in 1893. Meyer's film opens with a note-perfect homage to the 1960 George Pal film, as Wells (Malcolm McDowell) gathers his colleagues to announce his intention to travel through time. One guest, Dr. John Leslie Stevenson (David Warner) is late in arriving, as he has been busy murdering a prostitute in an alley. Yes, Dr. Stevenson is Jack the Ripper, a fact that comes to light when the police search the house and find bloodstained gloves in Stevenson's bag. It's too late, however, as the Ripper has already made his escape through time.

Wells pursues Stevenson into the future—specifically, the San Francisco of November 5, 1979. (November 5 is a significant date in time-travel history, as it's also the day Marty McFly arrives in 1955 in *Back to the Future*.) While attempting to track the Ripper down, Wells falls for a kindhearted bank teller (Mary Steenburgen), even as he comes to realize that the world of the future isn't the utopia he'd envisioned. Meyer's film is a terrifically entertaining, expertly blended mix of science fiction, comedy, romance, and thrills. McDowell, so often typecast in villainous roles, makes a delightfully sweet-natured, slightly bumbling fish out of water as Wells, and he and Steenburgen have all the chemistry you'd expect from a couple that fell in love on the set and later married. Stevenson is more of a plot device than a fleshed-out character, but Warner is appropriately menacing (even if the sight of Jack the Ripper stalking a disco in a jean vest and bell bottoms is more jarringly dated than the Victorian scenes).

Using time travel as a crime-fighting tool is all well and good, but more importantly, what are the military applications? For answers we turn to 1980's *The Final Countdown*, in which a freak electrical storm creates a space-time wormhole that sends the aircraft carrier USS *Nimitz* back to a few hours before December 7, 1941, not yet known as Pearl Harbor Day. Ignoring the possibility that intervention might delay the U.S. entry into World War II and perhaps result in a Nazi victory, the ship's captain (Kirk Douglas) reasons that his orders from the navy don't allow for such nuances as which decade it may or may not happen to be, so it's damn the torpedoes and full speed ahead. But before they have the chance to act, the wormhole reappears and sends the *Nimitz* back to the present. It all seems fairly pointless, until we learn that one crewman was left behind in the past and that he is the man who designed the *Nimitz* in the first place. Yes, it's another temporal paradox that will make your brain hurt if you think about it for too long.

Other notable time-travel films of the era include the 1980 romance *Somewhere in Time*, in which Christopher Reeve hypnotizes himself into the past to meet his true love; Terry Gilliam's cheeky 1981 fantasy *Time Bandits*, about a young boy who inadvertently joins a group of six dwarves using a map of the space-time continuum to loot various historical eras; and the 1986 sequel *Star Trek IV: The Voyage Home* (co-written by Nicholas Meyer), in which the crew of the *Enterprise* saves the whales by traveling back to 1980s San Francisco. But the most successful and beloved time-travel movie of the era is undoubtedly 1985's *Back to the Future*.

Written by Robert Zemeckis and Bob Gale, and directed by Zemeckis, this sci-fi comedy would seem to have little in common with *The Terminator*, but they do share one major plot point. In *The Terminator*, Kyle Reese travels to the past in order to ensure the birth of the future leader of the resistance in the War Against the Machines. In *Back to the Future*, suburban teenager Marty McFly finds himself in the past and must ensure his *own* birth by playing matchmaker for his future parents.

The screenplay for *Back to the Future* is ingeniously constructed, but its story unfolds with elegant simplicity. Marty (Michael J. Fox, who replaced original star Eric Stoltz after five weeks of shooting had already been completed) is summoned to meet his eccentric scientist friend Doc Brown (Christopher Lloyd) at a nearby mall, where he is conducting an experiment in time travel using a specially modified DeLorean. (Originally, Zemeckis and Gale had envisioned a time machine resembling a refrigerator but changed it for fear of young children getting stuck inside the Frigidaire while attempting to send themselves back to ancient Bedrock.) The secret to time travel is the flux capacitor, which is powered by plutonium—in this case, plutonium Brown stole from Libyan terrorists. When the terrorists show up at the mall and gun Brown down, Marty makes his escape in the DeLorean and winds up back in 1955.

More accurately, he finds himself in a nostalgic movie version of 1955, where "Mr. Sandman" tinkles in the background while four gas-station attendants in crisp white uniforms rush out to service a customer's car. When Marty inadvertently changes the past by disrupting the chain of events that would have led his mother Lorraine (Lea Thompson) to fall for his father George (Crispin Glover), his own existence is threatened—and even worse, Marty finds himself the object of Lorraine's affections. Amusing (if safely PG-rated) Oedipal complications ensue as Marty and the 1955 version of Doc Brown attempt to find a way to repair the past and send Marty back to the future.

Back to the Future isn't perfect by any means; the humor is often broader than the barn Marty crashes through on arrival in 1955, and the scene in which whitebread Michael J. Fox invents rock 'n' roll to the delight of an all-black band comes off as racially patronizing despite its jokey intentions. But the characters and setting, both past and present, are endearing, the plotting and attention to detail are airtight, and the staging of the climactic sequence at the clock tower is giddy slapstick-suspense perfection.

When *Back to the Future* finished as the highest-grossing movie of 1985, a sequel became inevitable, but Gale and Zemeckis had backed themselves into a corner with the ending of the first film. Purely as a joke, the filmmakers had had Doc Brown appear in a souped-up, flying version of the DeLorean to pick up Marty and his girlfriend Jennifer and take them into the future to fix a problem with their as-yet-nonexistent children. Gale and Zemeckis didn't particularly want to pursue that storyline but didn't think the fans would be happy if they ignored the setup they'd created. Eventually, after discarding a plotline in which Marty traveled back to 1967, they turned out a script that would have made for one very long, expensive sequel. It took some convincing from Gale, Zemeckis, and their producer Steven Spielberg, but eventually Universal Pictures president Sidney Sheinberg made the Solomonic decision to cut the movie in half. The sequels would be shot concurrently, with *Back to the Future Part II* being released on November 22, 1989, and *Part III* following six months later.

Part II is awkward and disjointed, and it lacks the emotional core of the first installment, but it deserves some credit for being one of the weirdest movies ever to attain blockbuster status. It begins immediately where the first part left off, as Doc, Marty, and the entirely superfluous Jennifer (Elisabeth Shue) travel from 1985 to the far-off, futuristic year of 2015. (Gale and Zemeckis hang a lampshade on their blunder of including Jennifer on the ride by having Doc knock her unconscious and dump her in an alley. Maybe not their finest creative moment.) As is documented throughout this book, predicting the near future is never easy, but Zemeckis takes a largely comedic approach here, so that *Part II*'s 2015 basically looks like a more extreme version of the 1980s. (The most prescient touch is the nostalgic diner The Cafe '80s, with its on-the-nose decor made up of the decade's most disposable yet fetishized cultural detritus; the video waiters that mash up '80s icons Ronald Reagan and Michael Jackson with short-lived 8-bit superstar Max Headroom are particularly inspired.)

The middle section of *Part II* takes place in a dark, alternate version of 1985 caused by further tampering with the space-time continuum. Reminiscent of the portion of *It's a Wonderful Life* wherein Jimmy Stewart sees Bedford Falls as it would have been had he never been born, this grim section of the film includes the densest time-travel exposition of the trilogy, as Doc attempts to explain in layman's terms that each change made in the past creates a separate branch of reality. Those viewers confused by this turn of events must have been positively flummoxed by the third act, in which Marty returns to 1955 to set things right and narrowly avoids running into the version of himself from the first movie who is already attempting to repair the past. For Zemeckis, this was the primary appeal of *Part II*; it was a unique opportunity to do a sequel that actually interacts with the first movie in fun and surprising ways. The film has its flaws, but for time-travel buffs, it's probably the most interesting exploration of the subject ever attempted in a mainstream movie.

The third and final chapter in the trilogy is far less ambitious. The original script for the *Back to the Future* sequel—the one that was too long and too expensive to make—concluded with a trip to the Old West, so it's no surprise that *Part III* essentially plays like an epilogue to the first two movies. After another accident with the DeLorean, Doc finds himself in 1885, where he romances schoolmarm Mary Steenburgen while Marty (dressed in a Howdy Doody western outfit and calling himself Clint Eastwood) tries to help him avoid being gunned down in a duel. The climactic sequence in which Doc and Marty use a steam engine to power the DeLorean on one last trip through time is another giddy, masterful set piece, but overall *Part III* feels like an episode of *Back to the Future: The TV Series*.

After all their mucking about throughout the space-time continuum, it's a little startling when *Part III* ends with Doc Brown telling Marty and Jennifer that "your future isn't written yet." His words make much of the trilogy seem like a waste of time in retrospect, but in a way, he's only echoing what Sarah Connor said to Kyle Reese while they were waiting for the end of the world: "There's no fate but what we make for ourselves."

FIVE MIND-BENDING TIME-TRAVEL MOVIES

***La Jetée* (1962)**—Chris Marker's experimental short is one of the most unusual, innovative films ever made, but no less haunting for that fact. The story of *La Jetée* unfolds over twenty-eight minutes through a series of black-and-white still photographs, accompanied by oddly poetic narration and creepy French whispering. "This is the story of a man, marked by an image from his childhood," we are told. As a boy, while visiting the Orly Airport to watch planes take off and land, he saw a woman's face that has never left his memory. After a nuclear war, while living as a prisoner in the tunnels beneath Paris, he is subject to an experiment. Since the human race is doomed, mankind's only hope is to find a loophole in time "to summon the Past and the Future to the aid of the Present." The man finds himself back on the airport jetty from his childhood, where his fate catches up with him. Terry Gilliam based his own mind-bender of a time-travel movie, *12 Monkeys*, on Marker's film, but the original remains a singular, powerful viewing experience.

***Idaho Transfer* (1973)**—This odd counterculture artifact directed by Peter Fonda concerns a research group of young hippies stumbling onto the secret of time travel. Their government-sponsored matter-transference project has resulted in an unexpected side effect, as both objects and people can be sent fifty-six years into the future, bypassing an eco-crisis that has apparently wiped out the human population. (For reasons that may have more to do with marketing appeal than any plot function, the attractive young people must remove their pants before using the time machine.) Events conspire to scuttle the hoped-for youth-culture utopia of the future before it can even get started. The Craters of the Moon National Monument makes for an appropriately eerie setting, and the low-budget film maintains an unsettling mundane tone, laced with occasional trippiness (a quality amplified by a DVD release that appears to have been transferred directly from a third-generation VHS dub).

***Donnie Darko* (2001)**—Richard Kelly crafted a genuine cult object by fusing John Hughes–style high school angst with time-trippy science fiction (and, most importantly, a big scary bunny). Jake Gyllenhaal plays the title character, a teen troubled by apocalyptic visions. With the help of a book called *The Philosophy of Time Travel*, Donnie is able to reverse a catastrophe, but the consequences are extreme in this oddly seductive directorial debut.

***Primer* (2004)**—Shane Carruth's brain-tickling $7,000 feature debut calls to mind Homer Simpson's classic evaluation of *Twin Peaks*: "Brilliant! I have absolutely no idea what's going on." Carruth's DIY aesthetic is reflected in the movie's almost documentary-like approach to the story of two technobabble-spouting inventors who find that their homemade superconductivity device has an unexpected bonus feature: time travel. They quickly figure out that they can use this infernal machine to their advantage on the stock market, but when a business colleague stumbles upon the box and figures out what it does, all hell begins to break loose. Exactly how it does so is the subject of much conjecture, and nearly impossible to untangle on first viewing. It's a head-spinning paradox encompassing multiple timelines and numerous copies of the characters, all unfolding with a bare minimum of exposition. Complex and thought-provoking, *Primer* proves you don't need grandiose visuals and elaborate special effects to stimulate the imagination.

***Timecrimes* (2007)**—Quirky Spanish filmmaker Nacho Vigalondo doesn't quite outdo *Primer* with the temporal machinations of his debut feature, but *Timecrimes* is still an enjoyable head-spinner in its own right. When bird-watching middle-aged suburbanite Hector (Karra Elejalde) spots a woman taking her shirt off in the woods behind his house, he's drawn into what at first seems like a Hitchcockian mystery. But after Hector is attacked by a scissors-wielding stranger with a bloody bandage wrapped around his head and takes refuge in a nearby laboratory, events take a science-fictional turn. With the help of a befuddled lab assistant, Hector enters what appears to be the prototype for the Hot Tub Time Machine, only to emerge from it earlier the same day. It will not be his last trip through time, as the complications pile up and the versions of Hector multiply. Like Shane Carruth before him, Vigalondo makes the most of his budget limitations with sheer ingenuity and flashes of dark humor.

THE *PLANET OF THE APES* REBOOTS

Once the *Planet of the Apes* movies had run their course, the next logical step was to transfer the franchise to the small screen. The final theatrical installment, *Battle for the Planet of the Apes*, basically looked like television anyway, so it was no great leap to imagine an *Apes* television series, particularly once CBS started airing the movies to great ratings success. Rod Serling was the first to take a crack at developing the series for TV, authoring a pair of scripts that made a somewhat confusing attempt at maintaining continuity with the films. Writers Art Wallace and Anthony Wilson took over, producing a much more streamlined take on the material that CBS hoped would draw in a large audience at the family hour.

Much to the surprise of the network and producers, Roddy McDowall agreed to don the chimp makeup once again, this time as the impish, inquisitive Galen. Ron Harper and James Naughton were cast as Virdon and Burke, a typically '70s Starsky-and-Hutch pair of astronauts who crash through the time barrier and find themselves on a future Earth dominated by apes. (This revelation is a bit less spectacular than it was in the first movie; instead of coming upon the Statue of Liberty, the astronauts find a picture book with photos of New York in it.) By the end of the first episode, "Escape from Tomorrow," Virdon, Burke, and Galen are all on the run from the ape authorities.

Following its premiere on September 13, 1974, the series quickly settled into a predictable format, with the trio of fugitives traveling from town to town, getting involved in some local drama, and trying to stay one step ahead of General Urko and his gorilla army. Nearly every week, Virdon, Burke, or Galen would get captured and the others would have to free him, narrowly escaping another encounter with Urko's forces in the process. Although the show was expensive to produce (largely due to the makeup), it didn't look like it, as the characters spent most of the episodes wandering around the same Malibu Canyon locations. Facing strong competition from *Sanford and Son* and *Chico and the Man*, *Planet* faltered in the ratings and was canceled after just fourteen episodes.

A year later, NBC made its own attempt at taking *Planet of the Apes* to weekly television, this time as a Saturday-morning cartoon series. Overseen by cartoonist Doug Wildey, *Return to the Planet of the Apes* was actually a much more ambitious show than its live-action predecessor. As in the original Pierre Boulle novel, this ape world is a technologically advanced one, complete with cars, planes, and televisions. Unlike the formulaic CBS series, *Return* endeavored to tell a continuing story that built dramatically from episode to episode—a rarity in children's television. The opening episode, "Flames of Doom," featured a witty reversal of the famous Statue of Liberty scene, as the astronauts stumbled upon a Mount Rushmore with four ape faces. Unfortunately, the animation was absolutely abysmal, even by the lax standards of '70s Saturday-morning fare. In many scenes, it's a challenge to spot anything moving at all. The voice acting is substandard, as well, which is a shame, as the series could have used some energy in performance to distract from the flat visuals. If only the creative team from the cartoon had been in charge of the live-action show, something good might have come of *Apes* on television. As it is, the animated series was just as short-lived as its predecessor.

A return to the big screen was inevitable but not easily achieved, even though some heavy hitters took a crack at it over the years. In 1992, Peter Jackson pitched a sequel that would have picked up the story after *Battle*, with Roddy McDowall returning yet again, this time as an elderly, da Vinci–esque chimp leading an artistic renaissance. A change in the 20th Century Fox hierarchy scuttled those plans, but *Apes* rose again two years later with Oliver Stone on board as producer. Stone's concept for the film, perhaps influenced by listening to too many Doors albums, involved "cryogenically frozen Vedic Apes who hold the secret numeric codes to the Bible that foretold the end of civilization." The project got as far as pre-production, but when it became clear that Fox wanted something closer in spirit to *The Flintstones*, it collapsed. The next big-name director to find his name linked to an *Apes* reboot was none other than James Cameron, who planned to cast Arnold Schwarzenegger in the lead. That certainly would have been a project of some interest to readers of this book, but of course, it never happened.

When a "re-imagining" of *Planet of the Apes* finally went into production in 2000, it was with *Batman* and *Beetlejuice* director Tim Burton at the helm. Burton had resisted a remake but changed his mind when he read the screenplay by William Broyles, which took the *Apes* saga in a new direction. Unfortunately, filming that script as written would have cost upward of $200 million, so pages were slashed and rewrites continued right up through production. The writing has traditionally been the weakest aspect of most Burton films, and *Apes* proves no exception, as whatever grand concepts Broyles may have envisioned are reduced to a feature-length chase sequence. Burton has admitted in interviews that his primary attraction to the material was all about the surfaces—the look, movements, and behavior of the apes—and on that level, his film is clearly superior to its predecessors. The makeup by Rick Baker is remarkable, and Tim Roth in particular conveys a ferocity and unpredictability as chimp General Thade.

Storywise, however, the Burton version is a bust. Astronaut Mark Wahlberg follows his trained chimp into an electromagnetic storm and is zapped through a wormhole to the titular planet. (For the first time since Boulle's original book, it's actually a different planet, not a future Earth.) The first appearance of the apes lacks any dramatic impact, and Wahlberg has no particular reaction to finding himself on a simian-dominated world. He might as well have gotten off at the wrong subway stop. Wahlberg is a bland presence throughout, but it's not entirely his fault, as he hasn't been given a compelling character to perform. Jokey references to the earlier films abound—Charlton Heston even makes a cameo in chimp makeup to reenact his "Damn them all to hell!" speech—as do jarring one-liners, like Paul Giamatti's orangutan lamenting, "Can't we all just get along?" In an attempt at replicating the original film's Statue of Liberty finale, the Burton version ends with a visual destined to leave audiences befuddled, as Wahlberg returns to Earth to find himself surrounded by gorillas in police uniforms at a Lincoln Memorial transformed into a monument to General Thade. Burton has said he intended this ending to leave the door open for a sequel, assuming Fox would want one, but although his film was a moneymaker, the franchise went dormant for another decade.

It resurfaced in 2011 as *Rise of the Planet of the Apes*, described by some as a prequel to the original film, and by others as a loose remake of *Conquest of the Planet of the Apes*. Thanks in part to James Cameron's efforts on *Avatar*, computer imagery and motion-capture technology had now advanced to the point where the apes could be created digitally while still maintaining a basis in human performance. Andy Serkis, the pioneering motion-capture actor who played Gollum in the *Lord of the Rings* trilogy and King Kong in the Peter Jackson remake, stars as Caesar, a modern-day chimp who becomes super-intelligent when genetic scientist James Franco tests an experimental Alzheimer's cure on him. After a violent incident, Caesar is confined to a run-down ape sanctuary, where he leads a revolt of his fellow primates that climaxes with a spectacular battle on the Golden Gate Bridge. The most entertaining *Apes* entry in nearly four decades, *Rise* is also the first successful reboot of the franchise, as a follow-up is in the works as of this writing.

Mel Gibson as Mad Max in the *The Road Warrior*.
(Kennedy Miller Productions/Warner Bros./Photofest)

5

HASTA LA VISTA, BABY: POST-APOCALYPTIC CINEMA

ATOMIC ANXIETY

As discussed in Chapter One, science-fiction films of the 1950s tended to address the post–World War II fears of the atom bomb through fantastical means. Radioactive fallout was to blame for the giant ants of *Them!*, *The Incredible Shrinking Man*, and Godzilla and all his associates from Japanese cinema. Films dealing head-on with the potential real-life consequences of a nuclear holocaust, on the other hand, were few and far between. The first such movie was 1951's *Five*, an independent production written, produced, and directed by Arch Oboler.

Oboler had made his name in radio drama, earning great acclaim for his work on the horror anthology series *Lights Out*. (Oboler wrote the famous episode *Chicken Heart*, which later became the basis of a Bill Cosby comedy routine.) Unfortunately, the talky and visually undistinguished *Five* suggests that Oboler should have stuck to radio. The film's title refers to the five survivors of a nuclear holocaust who happen to congregate at the same small house on a hill. They represent a cross-section of society: a tour guide from New York, a pregnant housewife, an elderly banker, a working-class black man, and a haughty adventurer. Will they take this apocalyptic opportunity to form a new society, free of the fears and prejudices that proved so destructive, or is it human nature that they make all the same mistakes again?

For all its dramatic deficiencies, *Five* should be credited (or blamed) for providing a template that's still the default setting for post-apocalyptic drama more than six decades later. As has so often been the case, Roger Corman was the first to tap the premise for its exploitation potential, with one of his earliest efforts as a producer and director, 1955's *Day the World Ended.* "I tried to make it something of a psychological study of a small group of people thrown together under unusual circumstances," Corman wrote in his memoir. But in truth, the movie plays more like Corman saw *Five* and thought, "Well, that's not bad, but wouldn't it be better if a radioactive, three-eyed mutant showed up halfway through?" This is why he's a national treasure, folks.

Required reading for anyone who attended high school between the Cuban Missile Crisis and the fall of the Berlin Wall, Nevil Shute's 1957 novel *On the Beach* depicted the aftermath of a nuclear war in grim, hopeless detail. (It's telling that this book kept being foisted on each successive generation, as if to say, "Well, we've utterly failed to solve this problem! Maybe we can scare you youngsters into doing something about it.") Inevitably, the king of the message movies, Stanley Kramer, adapted *On the Beach* for film in 1959.

As Kramer's film opens, an atomic war has seemingly wiped out life everywhere on the planet, save Australia and New Zealand. An American nuclear submarine commanded by Gregory Peck arrives in Melbourne, whose residents are living on borrowed time; sooner or later, the deadly cloud of radioactive fallout will reach its shores. The clock is ticking, but Kramer's film lacks all urgency, opting instead for standard Hollywood melodrama. Peck becomes embroiled in a love triangle with floozy Ava Gardner and scientist/drunkard/race car enthusiast Fred Astaire, while young sailor Anthony Perkins agonizes over abandoning his family in order to fulfill his military obligations. *On the Beach* has its isolated highlights, as in an emotional sequence wherein a crewman abandons ship in San Francisco Bay in order to spend his final days in the irradiated shell of his boyhood home, but for the most part, it's dreary soap opera right up until its admittedly powerful final moments.

Ultimately, *On the Beach* is a story of denial—of people going through the motions of their ordinary lives, long past the point of no return. Despite its fatalistic narrative arc, it's almost absurdly optimistic in its belief that human beings will continue to conduct themselves in accordance with societal norms after it all breaks down. In sharp contrast, 1962's *Panic in Year Zero!* depicts the rapid unraveling of the social fabric in the wake of a nuclear attack on the United States. Directed by Ray Milland, who also stars as a patriarch who will stop at nothing to keep his family secure, *Panic* is a taut, nasty little piece of work that would ultimately prove far more influential than its big-budget Hollywood counterpart. Later post-apocalyptic films will use the genre to explore what happens when all the rules have gone by the wayside. When civilization as we know it disintegrates, what social order (or disorder) rises in its wake?

THE DYSTOPIAN SEVENTIES

The political turbulence and social upheaval of the late 1960s was not immediately reflected in the mainstream movie making of the day. Hollywood is always slow to respond to cultural change, and it took the unexpected success of the independently produced *Easy Rider* to get the studio suits to notice the whiff of revolution in the air. As had been the case in the 1950s, science fiction proved an ideal medium for exploring the sort of "What if?" scenarios that the changing times churned up in the popular imagination.

Having single-handedly finished off the planet of apes (or so he thought), Charlton Heston signed on for another post-apocalyptic outing in *The Omega Man*, director Boris Sagal's 1971 adaptation of the Richard Matheson novel *I Am Legend*. Matheson's story had already reached the screen once before, in the 1964 Vincent Price vehicle *The Last Man on Earth*. A key influence on George Romero's *Night of the Living Dead*, that film starred Price as a scientist who survives a plague that has turned the rest of humanity into slow-moving (and slow-witted) vampires. Although initially successful at establishing an eerie mood, *Last Man* is ultimately undone by its budget deficiencies and the ridiculous ease with which its weak antagonists are defeated.

Omega Man takes a different approach, one far removed from anything Matheson could have envisioned when writing the novel. Here, post-apocalyptic Los Angeles is the final battleground in the war between The Man (embodied, of course, by square-jawed NRA spokesman Heston) and the counterculture (represented by the plague victims—black-robed albino hippies and Black Panther types, echoing the Manson cult by calling themselves "The Family"). Having survived the plague thanks to an experimental vaccine, Heston's Dr. Robert Neville whiles away his days attending repeat screenings of *Woodstock*, where he mockingly mouths along with the hippie platitudes expressed from the stage, and holes up at night in a penthouse apartment decorated in the finest early '70s swank. He is the one percent . . . or, more accurately, the .00001 percent.

He's not completely alone among the living, however, and the film takes a weird swerve toward conciliation when Neville hooks up with an Angela Davis lookalike who leads a small band of survivors. Interracial romance was still an onscreen rarity at the time, so credit the movie with progressive intent on at least one front, but this pairing is so unlikely, it could only happen if they were the last two people on Earth. Which, of course, they basically are. (Heston would revisit the dystopian realm of science fiction again in 1973's *Soylent Green*, playing a detective in an overpopulated future New York. This rather dull procedural is best known for its climactic and much-parodied revelation that "soylent green is people.")

Odd as *The Omega Man* is (and it's pretty much the ideal movie for bleary-eyed channel surfers to stumble upon at 2:00 a.m.), it pales in comparison to the lunacy unleashed in *A Boy and His Dog*. Based on a novella by Harlan Ellison (there he is again), and directed by L. Q. Jones, best known for his acting in the films of Sam Peckinpah, this 1975 cult film is both hugely influential and one of a kind. First, the influential part: *A Boy and His Dog* is the first of the post-apocalyptic films to appropriate the iconography of the western—which makes sense, given the director's background in oaters. The lone wanderer of the wilderness, the roving gangs preying on the weak, the makeshift settlements sprouting out of the desert landscape—all of these elements would have enormous impact on *The Road Warrior* and, by extension, its many imitators.

It's in the particulars of its story that *A Boy and His Dog* carves out its own inimitable niche in the post-apocalyptic landscape. Vic (a youthful Don Johnson) roams the devastated American wasteland of 2024, nearly two decades after the nuclear holocaust of World War IV. Despite his baby face, however, Vic is no innocent; he seeks only food, shelter, and women to rape. He is accompanied in his quest by his dog Blood, who communicates with him telepathically. Blood is clearly the brains of the outfit, a point made explicitly clear when Vic ignores the dog's pleading and follows a woman with whom he is smitten into "Down Under." This underground society is a perversion of small-town '50s America, where everyone wears whiteface and decisions of life and death are made by a three-person committee. Vic is informed that he's been led there in order to impregnate the women, which strikes him as a fine idea until he is hooked up to a milking mechanism designed to forcibly extract his sperm. While attempting to escape, he encounters an overalls-clad enforcer robot nearly as unstoppable as the Terminator.

Consistently bizarre and only occasionally repellent, *A Boy and His Dog* is one of the most twisted, original visions of the apocalyptic future ever realized on film, despite the fact that it was made on a very small budget, with few special effects and minimal production design. By contrast, 1976's *Logan's Run* was a major studio release and one of the most lavish sci-fi productions of the pre–*Star Wars* era. Directed by Michael Anderson, the film was based on a 1967 novel by William F. Nolan and George Clayton Johnson, which drew inspiration from the youth movement of its era in its depiction of a future dystopian society.

In the novel, the sit-ins and protests of the 1960s sired a youth-dominated society, one that gained the force of law once overpopulation raged out of control. By 2116, a maximum age of twenty-one is being enforced by officers known as Sandmen, who are charged with hunting down and killing runners—those who have failed to comply with the mandatory death sentence. One of these Sandmen, Logan 3, becomes a runner himself in order to infiltrate the underground network helping runners to escape, but when he falls for fellow runner Jessica 6, he abandons his mission for the cause of his own survival. The novel is a briskly paced read that uses its chase structure to unveil the layers of a beguiling future world, and is highly recommended.

In the 1976 film, the maximum age was raised to thirty in order to facilitate casting, most notably Michael York as Logan and Jenny Agutter as Jessica. An opening title card informs us that in the twenty-third century, "survivors of war, overpopulation and pollution are living in a great domed city, sealed away from the forgotten world outside." Here mankind lives only for pleasure, and the powerful central Computer provides all. In another fuzzy-minded change from the book, those who have reached the age of thirty participate in "Carousel", a sort of Cirque du Soleil act that supposedly provides the opportunity for "renewal" but in practice seems to result only in people exploding.

Otherwise, the first half of the film is a reasonably faithful adaptation of the book, and particularly enjoyable for fans of retro '70s futurism. Predominantly shot in a Fort Worth shopping mall, the domed city of *Logan's Run* spruces up the usual gleaming white corridors of the future with a bedizened disco-ball aesthetic. Like the visuals, the pulsing synth score by Jerry Goldsmith occupies the intersection of creepy and cheesy, and while the special effects tend to be clunky, they, too, possess a certain vintage charm. (The android Box, a fearsome Terminator-like cyborg in the novel, here becomes Roscoe Lee Browne in a rolling tube of tinfoil, extolling the virtues of "fish, and plankton, and sea greens, and protein from the sea.")

Once Logan and Jessica make their escape from the domed city, the movie departs from its source material and loses its way. While the novel postulates a sort of underground railroad for runners leading to an actual Sanctuary—an abandoned space station near Mars—the movie offers Peter Ustinov as a doddering old man surrounded by his cats in the ruins of Washington, D.C. Given that this foolish character is the first exposure Logan and Jessica have ever had to a person over thirty, it's unclear why the idea of growing older would continue to have any appeal to them. Nevertheless, Logan returns to the domed city, where he uses the Captain Kirk "logic bomb" technique to confuse the almighty Computer and free the citizens from their pampered lives of luxury. How these people who have had their every need catered to all their lives are going to survive longer than a week in the wild is anybody's guess.

DAWN OF THE DEAD: ROMERO'S ZOMBIE APOCALYPSE

Of course, *Logan's Run* wasn't the only post-apocalyptic '70s movie filmed primarily inside a shopping mall. George Romero hadn't planned to make a sequel to his seminal zombie film *Night of the Living Dead*, but an idea came to him while taking a tour of the then-new Monroeville Mall near his home base of Pittsburgh. Part-owner Mark Mason showed Romero some behind-the-scenes areas of the mall, including hidden rooms stocked with civil-defense supplies. When Mason offhandedly remarked that a hermit could survive a long time hidden away in there, Romero's thoughts turned back to the living dead.

In the mid- to late 1970s, large indoor shopping centers weren't nearly as ubiquitous as they would become (which is probably why *Logan's Run* could get away with using one as the city of the future), but Romero saw potential in the setting for a consumerist satire in the guise of a horror movie. As *Dawn* begins, the zombie epidemic that began in *Night of the Living Dead* is now starting to completely overwhelm society's ability to control it. Two surviving members of a SWAT team sent into a tenement swarming with the living dead decide they've had enough, and plan to escape the city in a helicopter along with its pilot and his girlfriend. After passing over countryside teeming with zombies (along with redneck hunters whooping it up as they blast holes in the living dead-heads), the chopper sets down on the roof of the Monroeville Mall.

The four survivors set up camp inside the civil-defense area of the mall, then set about clearing the shopping center of all its zombie inhabitants and sealing off all the entrances. Once they've established the mall as a safe zone, it becomes their own personal playground, as they begin to enact a simulation of real life within its walls. Ignoring the problem works for only so long, but it is telling that it's not zombies but other people (in the form of a marauding biker gang) who represent the real threat to their security.

In contrast to the stark black-and-white horrors of *Night of the Living Dead*, Romero adopts an admittedly comic-bookish tone for *Dawn*, employing garish colors and cranking up the comedic aspects of his scenario. That's not to say the violence has been toned down—heads explode, intestines are spilled, and flesh is ripped and devoured at regular intervals—but the emphasis here is less on sustained terror than on social commentary. Far from being dated, Romero's satire is probably more relevant now than at the time of the movie's release. These days, you hardly need Romero's help if you want to see hordes of mindless zombies overrunning shopping malls; recent years have seen news reports of "Black Friday" consumer mob violence that could easily be mistaken for outtakes from *Dawn*.

It should be noted that there's nothing heavy-handed about Romero's satiric approach here; on one level, the mall is simply an amusing and colorful location for a zombie takeover. At one point, the director stages a sort of slapstick ballet set to Muzak, as the living dead tumble down escalators, trip over furniture, and fall face-first into the fountain. But despite these lighthearted moments, *Dawn* never loses its undercurrent of dread and pervasive sense of loss as civilization is stripped away, leaving only its material residue behind.

Romero would complete his original *Living Dead* trilogy with 1985's *Day of the Dead*, but as it turned out, that was only the beginning. It took a while, but eventually "zombie apocalypse" became a genre unto itself, spawning such films as *28 Days Later*, *Zombieland*, and Zack Snyder's 2004 remake of *Dawn of the Dead*. The AMC network, home of prestige fare like *Mad Men* and *Breaking Bad*, adapted Robert Kirkman's Romero-influenced comic book *The Walking Dead* as a weekly television series and saw it become a pop-culture phenomenon. Romero got back in the game, as the man who started it all directed three more *Living Dead* installments: *Land of the Dead*, *Diary of the Dead*, and *Survival of the Dead*. The Max Brooks novel *World War Z* became a bestseller destined for the big screen, and even the Centers for Disease Control got in on the action, releasing a preparedness guide to the zombie apocalypse. That last item might have been tongue-in-cheek (or, in zombie terms, tongue-through-cheek), but its underlying purpose was deadly serious. While an actual zombie apocalypse might be a long shot, the threat of a devastating worldwide pandemic is always lurking.

THE STAND: DOOMSDAY À LA KING

George Romero originally intended to follow up *Dawn of the Dead* with an adaptation of Stephen King's 1978 novel *The Stand*. In fact, the first paperback edition of the book carried a line on the cover reading, "Soon to be a major motion picture directed by George Romero." The development phase of the project dragged on throughout the '80s, with King himself churning out a 400-page script at one point, but the same problem kept cropping up: the book simply had too much story for a single motion picture to handle at a reasonable running time.

After finishing *The Shining*, King had begun work on a *roman à clef* about the Patty Hearst kidnapping, but, in a rarity for the prolific author, he was making no headway. One day he read a news report about a chemical/biological warfare test that went awry in Utah, killing many sheep in the process. "But," King wrote in his breezy survey of the horror genre, *Danse Macabre*, "the news article stated, if the wind had been blowing the other way, the good people of Salt Lake City might have gotten a very nasty surprise." The incident reminded him of a post-apocalyptic novel by George R. Stewart called *The Earth Abides*, in which much of the Earth's population was killed off by a virulent disease. King felt Stewart's book got too bogged down in ecological issues, but the basic premise stuck with him. He shifted his focus to a new novel, which began with a strain of superflu known as "Captain Trips" wiping out 99.4% of the Earth's population.

The first section of the book follows the spread of the virus, which begins when a soldier escapes from a quarantined army base where a biological weapon is being tested. In the second section, the few survivors are drawn to one of two outposts of humanity: the "Free Zone" of Boulder, Colorado, where the followers of saintly

Mother Abigail congregate, and city of sin Las Vegas, where the minions of "Dark Man" Randall Flagg conspire. The final section details the confrontation between these two factions, which, like many of King's early works, builds to a literally explosive finale.

The first of King's epic-length novels, and the one most deserving of the doorstop-sized treatment, *The Stand* has proven to be one of the most influential works of the last half century. Its high-stakes battle of good and evil was an oft-acknowledged inspiration for producers Carlton Cuse and Damon Lindelof in their plotting of the cult hit series *Lost*, and the many post-apocalyptic series that followed (see sidebar) certainly took their cue from King's magnum opus. The 2010 bestseller *The Passage*, by Justin Cronin, is unimaginable without the King novel.

The George Romero version of *The Stand* will forever remain one of those mythical lost projects, like Alejandro Jodorowsky's *Dune* or David Lynch's *Return of the Jedi*. In 1994, a TV miniseries based on *The Stand* aired on ABC, and although it had its moments (notably the opening sequence cued to Blue Oyster Cult's "Don't Fear the Reaper"), the network version was inevitably watered down and disappointing. In 2011, it was announced that actor/director Ben Affleck would tackle a new big-screen version of *The Stand* for Warner Bros.

THE DAY AFTER: COLD WAR NIGHTMARES OF THE REAGAN AGE

In the early to mid-1980s, nuclear paranoia reached a level unseen since the Cuban Missile Crisis. The Soviet Union had invaded Afghanistan in 1979, setting the stage for a heightening of tensions between the two superpowers. The 1980 election of Ronald Reagan, a hard-line Cold Warrior who would refer to the USSR as "the Evil Empire" in speeches, only intensified the frightening possibility of global thermonuclear warfare. Even purple party-pop star Prince was singing, "Everybody's got a bomb, we could all die any day." The overwhelming sense of helplessness in the face of potential destruction is perhaps one reason *The Terminator* struck such a chord in 1984. Here was a story in which an ordinary person could make a difference and potentially avert disaster. Few other apocalypse-themed works of the time were as optimistic.

On a November night in 1983, one of the largest American television audiences of all time—nearly 100 million total viewers—tuned into the ABC network to watch a movie of the week unlike any other. Written by television veteran Edward Hume and directed by Nicholas Meyer (*Time After Time*), *The Day After* depicted a nuclear attack and its aftermath through the prism of Lawrence, Kansas. The cast included Jason Robards, JoBeth Williams, John Lithgow, and Steve Guttenberg (a long way from *Police Academy*).

Although ABC had originally intended to air the film over two nights, they made the decision to condense it into a single evening's viewing by airing it without commercial interruption following the nuclear attack. (Apparently at least one wise executive realized that viewers wouldn't be in the mood to see the Ty-D-Bol Man after witnessing such cataclysmic destruction.) The original airing of the film was followed by a studio discussion that included Dr. Carl Sagan, Henry Kissinger, and Robert McNamara.

The Day After was undoubtedly a one-of-a-kind television event and may have even had a positive impact on U.S. policy. After watching the inaugural airing, Ronald Reagan wrote in his diary, "It's very effective and left me greatly depressed." Hollywood veteran Reagan was always strongly influenced by movies, and many believe his viewing of *The Day After* played a role in his signing of the Intermediate-Range Nuclear Forces Treaty in Reykjavík three years later. If there's any truth to that, then *The Day After* certainly succeeded as a polemic, as well as a cultural event. Whether it actually succeeds as drama is another matter.

Seen today, the movie is perhaps inevitably tainted with the trappings of its time. For its first hour it plays very much like a standard '80s movie of the week, and while this may have worked in its favor at the time (lulling people into a state of complacency before whacking them over the head), now it just feels dated. The same goes for the special effects during the attack scene, most notably the cheesy "x-ray" flashes used to depict people being vaporized by the bomb. The idyllic heartland imagery of the first hour, with its churches and ball fields and families playing horseshoes, is so overstated as to be corny. Still, *The Day After* was never really intended to be judged on the usual aesthetic terms; it set out to make a point, and did so successfully.

Appearing nearly simultaneously with *The Day After* was *Testament*, originally produced for PBS but accorded a small theatrical run at the end of 1983. In fact, "the PBS version of *The Day After*" is probably the best shorthand way to describe the gentle domestic apocalypse that unfolds in *Testament*. Lynne Littman's film takes place in the fictional San Francisco suburb of Hamlin, which is initially undamaged when the bombs fall. (Our only sight of the nuclear holocaust is a bright flash of light through the curtains of a living room window.) Littman's focus is on a mother (Jane Alexander) left to raise her children alone for whatever weeks of their lives remain, after her husband (William Devane) is killed in the blast. The external factors may not be starkly realistic, but the emotional turmoil is vividly felt, and Littman brings a rare but welcome feminine perspective to the issue.

For a take on the subject that pulls absolutely no punches, look no further than *Threads*, a 1984 BBC telefilm that makes *The Day After* look like a Disney cartoon. Unsparingly bleak and brutal, *Threads* was partially inspired by *The War Game*, a pseudo-documentary that director Peter Watkins had made for the BBC in 1965. Although the BBC had approved Watkins' script, they refused to show the completed film, which went unaired for two decades. Written by Barry Hines and directed by Mick Jackson, *Threads* incorporates elements of Watkins' documentary style with kitchen-sink realism to tell a story that runs along parallel lines with *The Day After*, to startlingly more gut-wrenching effect. It's a brilliant film that's impossible to imagine watching more than once.

While *The Day After* unfolds in the American Midwest, setting up a stark contrast between pre-nuclear pastoral idyll and post-nuclear wreckage, *Threads* is centered on Sheffield, an industrial outpost in Northern England that, at least in the early 1980s, already exuded an air of bombed-out despair. The run-up to the nuclear attack plays out in the background, on televisions, radios, and newspaper headlines, as a young working-class couple deals with the seemingly life-and-death issue of an unexpected pregnancy. The film's scope expands outward (the "threads" of the title are those of the social fabric) as the clock winds to zero hour and the nukes reduce the city to rubble. With pitiless clarity, *Threads* traces the progression of events, from initial radioactive fallout to nuclear winter to the near-medieval civilization existing more than a decade after the attack. *The Day After* ends with the joyful birth of a newborn and Jason Robards getting a hug. *Threads* also ends with a birth, but the baby is deformed and stillborn. The only mercy shown by the filmmakers is to freeze the frame and cut to black before the mother's shriek of horror.

Those who are not quite up for such a harrowing experience may want to check out the 1982 documentary *The Atomic Cafe* instead. Made up entirely of newsreel footage and archival clips from government and military films, and scored to some of the catchiest atomic-themed ditties of the '40s and '50s, *Cafe* takes a rather cheeky approach to showcasing the horrors of the nuclear age. By juxtaposing the apocalyptic images of actual bomb tests and the after-effects of the Hiroshima and Nagasaki blasts with laughably inadequate instructional films, this documentary by Jayne Loader, Kevin Rafferty, and Pierce Rafferty exposes the unbreachable gulf between the destructive power of our weapons and the banal platitudes we employ to feel better about them. This is how we learned to stop worrying and love the bomb.

THE ROAD WARRIOR AND OTHER WANDERERS OF THE WASTELAND

George Miller's debut feature *Mad Max* arrived in 1979 as part of a wave of colorful and creative drive-in pictures produced in Australia. (These films have collectively come to be known as "Ozploitation," and you can learn more about them in the terrifically entertaining retrospective documentary *Not Quite Hollywood*.) Miller's film was a nasty little revenge thriller set in a vaguely dystopian future, starring a then-unknown Mel Gibson (whose name would become practically synonymous with "revenge thrillers" before it became synonymous with "crazy off-screen behavior"). The movie's high-octane automotive carnage helped make it the highest-grossing movie ever in Australia at the time of its release, but *Mad Max* did nothing in America, partially thanks to a crude and unnecessary dubbing job that gave the perfectly understandable English-speaking characters goofy American accents.

Mad Max remains an exciting B movie, but even its hardcore fans must have been flabbergasted by the upgrades Miller made for its sequel two years later. *Mad Max* took place in a world that could best be described as pre-apocalyptic; the civilization it depicted was on the brink and beset by lawlessness, but it was still a civilization. *Mad Max 2* (known as *The Road Warrior* in the United States, where the Mad Max name carried no weight at the time) opens with a narrator informing us that "two mighty warrior tribes went to war and touched off a blaze which engulfed them all." What remains, as far as we can see, is an every-man-for-himself wasteland, where fuel is the most scarce and desired of commodities.

Miller renders this future world as a masterful pop-art collision of spaghetti western landscapes, '70s gearhead-movie energy, and punk-rock style. As mentioned above, *The Road Warrio*r borrows liberally from *A Boy and His Dog*, but it borrows from a dozen other pop-culture influences, as well, from Kurosawa to Corman to comic books, distilling them all into one of the freshest, most exhilarating action pictures of all time. Miller keeps dialogue to a bare minimum, preferring to tell the story in purely visual terms whenever possible. (Gibson has the same number of lines of dialogue as Schwarzenegger in the first *Terminator*: sixteen.) For pure kinetic energy, its chase sequences are unparalleled, but *The Road Warrior* is also notable for the compelling post-apocalyptic world it depicts—a world that would prove enormously influential on a number of filmmakers, including James Cameron. The junkyard aesthetic of the post-apocalyptic scenes in *The Terminator* owes a debt to Miller's work, one that Cameron has acknowledged. "[W]hen I was writing *The Terminator*, *The Road Warrior* came out, and I said, 'This is the next step.'"

Kevin Costner certainly must have wished he'd played Mad

Max, as he twice attempted to replicate *The Road Warrior*, both times with disastrous results. *Waterworld* let the makers of *Ishtar* off the hook by becoming Hollywood's new shorthand for a runaway project doomed to box-office failure in 1995, while *The Postman* was virtually ignored two years later. Similar "wanderer of the wasteland" knockoffs continue to show up every so often in theaters, with 2010's *The Book of Eli*, starring Denzel Washington, being one of the more recent examples. One that might be of interest to fans of both Mad Max and the Terminator is 1990's *Hardware*, the debut feature from music-video director Richard Stanley. As was often the case with filmmakers making the transition from MTV to the big screen, Stanley proves better at crafting stylized eye candy than a coherent narrative, but Stacey Travis is eminently watchable as a woman who discovers her hidden resources of strength and ingenuity while battling a seemingly unstoppable killer robot. (Sound familiar?)

George Miller himself returned to the post-apocalyptic world he'd created in 1985's *Mad Max Beyond Thunderdome*, although this time he was only one of two credited directors. Miller primarily stuck to directing the action sequences, while George Ogilvie handled the dramatic scenes. Perhaps because of this split, *Thunderdome* is at its best in the early scenes set in the frontier outpost Bartertown, and in the chase sequence that ends the picture. As we've learned with the Terminator, however, no good sci-fi franchise ever really dies; it just goes dormant for a while. As of 2012, the long-delayed fourth Mad Max film, *Fury Road*, was finally set to go before the cameras, with Tom Hardy taking over the lead role. It's said to be the first film in a new trilogy, but, as always, the box office will have the final say on that matter.

APOCALYPSE HOW? FIVE OFFBEAT ENDS OF THE WORLD AS WE KNOW IT

***Gas-s-s-s* (1971)**—An experimental gas escapes from a chemical research facility in Alaska, killing everyone on Earth over the age of twenty-five. Director Roger Corman described this fractured, DayGlo picaresque as a "Strangelovian comedy," but as its counterculture protagonists find themselves reenacting atrocities from American history in increasingly absurd fashion, it plays more like drive-in Godard. Inextricably tied to its time, *Gas-s-s-s* is still goofy, groovy fun and would make a great double bill with . . .

***Glen and Randa* (1971)**—Jim McBride (*David Holzman's Diary*) directed this obscurity from the waning days of the hippie era, set one generation after the fall of civilization (presumably due to nuclear war, as a mushroom cloud is prominently featured in the promotional artwork). The young, hairy, and oft-nude inhabitants of this world that nature has begun to reclaim must rely on artifacts like Rolling Stones records and Wonder Woman comics for their knowledge of how the world works, while the few remaining older people are either craven opportunists or harmless nutjobs. Rudy Wurlitzer, who seemingly had a hand in every counterculture-themed movie of the late '60s and early '70s, contributed to the screenplay of this uneven but worthwhile effort.

***Quintet* (1979)**—Leave it to Robert Altman to concoct the least appealing post-apocalyptic society this side of *Threads*. Set in a future Ice Age, *Quintet* is so white with snow and glare, you will notice hitherto imperceptible streaks of dust on your television screen. The remaining inhabitants of this dreary age reside in the ruins of some sort of sewage treatment plant or perhaps trendy industrial-style disco, and spend their spare time playing the bizarre and deadly game (invented by Altman) that gives the film its title. The game itself doesn't look like all that much fun, but since there's not much else to do besides club seals or freeze to death and get eaten by dogs, everyone plays it continuously anyway. *Quintet* certainly isn't one of Altman's classics, but those with a fondness for the director's weirder side (e.g., *Three Women*) will want to give it a try.

***Night of the Comet* (1984)**—When the Earth passes through the tail of a comet, most of the population is reduced to red dust. Survivors partially exposed to the comet are slowly turning into zombies, hunting the very few who were completely shielded from the rays, including teenage sisters Regina (Catherine Mary Stewart) and Samantha (Kelli Maroney). Writer/director Thom Eberhardt's cult favorite is pitched somewhere between *Valley Girl* and *Repo Man* on the scale of '80s New Wave comedies. Awash in pink neon, bad fashion, and chirpy synth-pop tunes on the soundtrack, it's undeniably a relic of its time, but that only adds to its goofy appeal.

***The Rapture* (1991)**—The biblical apocalypse has often figured into films aimed at a Christian audience, like *The Omega Code* and *Left Behind*, but Michael Tolkin's directorial debut is something else entirely. Mimi Rogers gives a career-best performance as a deadened directory-assistance operator who fills her spiritual void with a swinging sex life until her yearning for something more meaningful leads her to a religious conversion. Tolkin's film appears to be a psychological study of the dangers of fanaticism, until its final moments bring a literal Judgment Day, complete with the Four Horsemen of the Apocalypse. As in his uniquely disturbing novel *Among the Dead*, Tolkin finds original ways to unsettle and provoke at every turn.

APOCALYPTIC TELEVISION

Post-apocalyptic scenarios occasionally figured into episodes of *The Twilight Zone* and *The Outer Limits*, but for most of television history, the end of the world was not the stuff of weekly family-hour entertainment. One major exception aired from 1975 to 1977 on the BBC, which was certainly more likely to give such dark material a shot than the American television networks of the time. *Survivors* was conceived and written by Terry Nation, a BBC veteran best known for creating the Daleks on *Doctor Who*. The setup for the series is quickly dispatched in the opening-credits sequence, which depicts a Chinese scientist accidentally spilling a sample of a deadly virus, which he then spreads through his travels. As the opening episode, "The Fourth Horseman," begins, the pandemic is spreading throughout England and presumably the rest of the world. By the end of the first hour, it appears that only a handful of survivors remain in the London area. In subsequent episodes, Nation tackles the question of what sort of society will rise in the wake of the apocalypse, with one group striving to establish a self-sufficient agrarian commune of sorts, while another attempts to impose a totalitarian law-and-order regime.

Nation departed after the first year, but the series continued for two more seasons and was remade by the BBC in 2008. Aside from the rather dire Showtime series *Jeremiah*, however, post-apocalyptic television didn't really catch on as a trend until after the success of ABC's *Lost*. While *Lost* was not itself post-apocalyptic (although many fans initially theorized it might have been), it established that many of the tropes associated with post-apocalyptic fiction—survivalism, a disparate group of characters attempting to build a new society, the group splintering into factions—could translate to an ongoing television story.

Among the first wave of *Lost*-influenced TV series to hit the airwaves was CBS's *Jericho*, set in a fictional Kansas town of the same name. In the pilot episode, Jake Green (Skeet Ulrich) returns to his hometown of Jericho, having left five years earlier following a blow-up with his father. Shortly after his arrival, the United States is attacked with nuclear weapons, and Jericho effectively becomes cut off from the rest of the world. The first season mixed soap opera–style relationship storylines with more action-oriented survival drama, culminating in the discovery of another town of survivors, which ultimately declares war on Jericho. CBS initially canceled *Jericho* after the first season, citing declining ratings, but the show's fans rallied on the Internet, persuading the network to order an abbreviated second season of seven episodes. The second season focused on a repressive provisional government taking over Jericho and transforming it into a police state. *Jericho*'s ratings got even worse in its return to the airwaves, and the series was canceled for good. (A "season three" of sorts does exist in comic book form.)

The most successful post-apocalyptic television series from a ratings standpoint is AMC's *The Walking Dead*. Based on the comic books by Robert Kirkman and produced by *Shawshank Redemption* director Frank Darabont (at least until he left the series under mysterious circumstances between seasons one and two), the show draws heavily on George Romero's "living dead" mythology in its depiction of life in the aftermath of a zombie apocalypse. The story concerns a small-town Georgia deputy (Andrew Lincoln) who wakes from a coma after being shot in the line of duty and finds himself in a world overrun with flesh-eating "walkers." After catching up with a band of survivors, including his wife (Sarah Wayne Callies), son (Chandler Riggs), and former partner (Jon Bernthal), he leads them on a quest for survival, in hopes of finding some remnant of civilization safe from the walking dead. After a strong start, *The Walking Dead* has begun to show the limitations of ongoing series set in the post-apocalypse, as its second season slowly bogged down into a morass of static situations and unlikable characters. It ratings remained strong, however, suggesting that television is far from finished exploring post-apocalyptic scenarios.

Arnold Schwarzenegger in *Conan the Barbarian*. (Universal Pictures/Photofest)

6

MR. UNIVERSE: ARNOLD SCHWARZENEGGER'S BODY OF WORK

THE UNLIKELIEST SUPERSTAR

Even Harlan Ellison at his most imaginative could not have conceived the improbable rise of Arnold Schwarzenegger, from a small Austrian village to the heights of Hollywood stardom to the seat of power in the state of California. (Of course, if Ellison *had* conceived such a story, he would have sued Schwarzenegger for plagiarism by now.) Born in Thal, Austria, on July 30, 1947, to policeman and former Nazi brownshirt Gustav Schwarzenegger and his wife Aurelia, young Arnold grew up in a pastoral setting without many modern conveniences. The movie theater in nearby Graz opened his eyes to the wider world, with the aspiring bodybuilder drawn in particular to the films of Steve Reeves and Reg Park, both musclemen best known for playing Hercules.

Schwarzenegger built his physique to Charles Atlas proportions throughout his teenage years, competing in his first bodybuilding competition at age seventeen. While performing his mandatory year of military service, he went AWOL in order to compete internationally for the first time, winning the title of Junior Mr. Europe and a brief stay in the stockade for his efforts. By the age of twenty, he had been crowned Mr. Universe, a title grandiose enough to satiate almost any ego. Not Schwarzenegger's, however; not only had he outgrown his little Austrian town, but his dreams were too big to be contained by the entire continent of Europe. "Everything I wanted as a kid was American," he said, according to Nigel

Andrews' biography *True Myths*. "I hated everything about Austria—the classical music and the museums. I hated this old shit."

The American dream was beckoning, and Schwarzenegger pursued it with the same single-minded intensity he'd brought to sculpting his body. It must have seemed like all his Christmases had come at once when he was offered his first movie role: Hercules. Like his idols Reeves and Park before him, he would make the leap to the big screen, thanks to bodybuilding mogul Joe Weider, who assured the producers of 1969's *Hercules in New York* that Arnold was a Shakespearean stage actor in Europe. That was clearly not the case, and the film sank without a trace, postponing Schwarzenegger's Hollywood stardom for over a decade.

While appearing in minor muscleman roles in several films throughout the '70s (including Robert Altman's *The Long Goodbye*), he continued his competitive bodybuilding career, capturing Mr. Universe and Mr. Olympia titles along the way. His biggest shot at stardom came in 1977, when a documentary crew descended on Gold's Gym in Venice Beach, and Schwarzenegger didn't miss it. He lit up the resulting film *Pumping Iron* with a charisma and swagger his fellow bodybuilders couldn't hope to match. Hollywood came calling, although at first it seemed only two viable types of roles were available to him: bodybuilders and sword-and-sandals musclemen. That would all change when a young director every bit as ambitious as Schwarzenegger cast him as the Terminator and helped turn him into a one-name star: Ah-nuld.

The prospect of plodding chronologically through Arnold's oeuvre isn't terribly appealing, so in the interest of having a little more fun with it, what follows is a highly subjective ranking of the big man's top twenty movies (excluding the Terminator franchise), followed by a list of the five worst Schwarzenegger movies of all time.

THE TOP TWENTY (NON-*TERMINATOR*) ARNOLD SCHWARZENEGGER MOVIES

20. *Twins* (1988)—In an effort to broaden his appeal following his string of successful action pictures in the 1980s, Schwarzenegger teamed up with director Ivan Reitman (*Ghostbusters*) for the first of three high-concept comedies. The result is less fully-realized movie than 100-minute marketing hook. Like the exploitation hucksters of old, the Universal publicity department distilled their product's essence into an eye-catching one-sheet poster: Schwarzenegger and co-star Danny DeVito, dressed identically in late-'80s business casual, mugging under the one-word title TWINS. It's funny, you see, because Schwarzenegger and DeVito look nothing alike! That might be enough comedy to fuel a three-minute *Saturday Night Live* sketch, but one joke wears awfully thin at feature length. On the plus side, Arnold is oddly endearing as sweet-natured naïf Julius Benedict, the result of genetic experimentation designed to produce a physically and mentally advanced human being. When Julius discovers the experiment had the unintended result of producing a somewhat less advanced twin, he travels from the remote tropical island where he's spent his entire life to Los Angeles, where he meets his lowlife brother Vincent (DeVito, in his usual gruff vulgarian mode). The odd-couple pairing brings out the rank sentimentalist in Reitman, and his movie's mawkish attempts at tear-jerking far outnumber its genuine laughs. Audiences showed up in droves anyway, and Schwarzenegger's comedy career move proved to be a shrewd one.

The Trivial Arnold: After the box office success of *Twins*, a sequel entitled *Triplets*, in which Schwarzenegger and DeVito would be joined by a third sibling played by Roseanne Barr, was reported to be in the works. It never happened, but rumors of a sequel resurfaced as recently as the summer of 2011.

19. *The Jayne Mansfield Story* (1980)—Sadly, Schwarzenegger doesn't play the title role in this biopic of the pneumatic star of *The Girl Can't Help It* and *Will Success Spoil Rock Hunter?* That honor goes to Loni Anderson, who proves eminently capable of recreating Mansfield's "divoon" bubbleheaded blonde persona but fails to suggest the hidden depths this made-for-TV movie would like us to believe were concealed beneath that spectacular décolletage. Anderson's near-continual squealing may be accurate mimicry, but it's also the stuff of migraines. Schwarzenegger fares somewhat better as Mansfield's long-suffering husband, Hungarian bodybuilder Mickey Hargitay, but it's not as if he had much competition for the role. Schwarzenegger also serves as the movie's narrator, as Hargitay tells Mansfield's story to a reporter. When he talks about her nose for publicity and her belief that actors are really just "personalities frozen in amber," he might well be describing the superstar he's about to become.

The Trivial Arnold: In an otherwise scathing review in the *Washington Post*, critic Tom Shales wrote that Schwarzenegger "gives the movie a certain lunkheaded charm with his fractured phonetic line readings." High praise indeed.

18. *Collateral Damage* (2002)—After the terrorist attacks of 9/11, several films saw their release dates delayed as Hollywood allegedly wrestled with its place in a new era of responsible entertainment. That lasted about six months, before this thriller about a fireman seeking vengeance following the death of his wife and son in a terrorist bombing on U.S. soil was released. Badly miscast in a role tailor-made for a pre-scandal Mel Gibson, Schwarzenegger gives a glum performance, providing ample evidence that "dark and brooding" is nowhere to be found in his acting wheelhouse. There's a mildly intriguing twist involving the identity of the Colombian guerrilla villain of the piece, but *Collateral Damage* is mostly of interest to action fans who can't get enough of people running and jumping out of the way of gigantic fireballs.

The Quotable Arnold: "I'll show you collateral damage!"

17. *Kindergarten Cop* (1990)—The pitch meeting for the second in Schwarzenegger's trio of high-concept comedies with Ivan Reitman must have lasted all of six seconds. What more would a Hollywood executive need to hear than "Arnold Schwarzenegger IS Kindergarten Cop"? Those five words conjure the whole movie, in which Arnold plays a gritty L.A. cop who goes undercover as a substitute teacher in an Oregon kindergarten in order to track down the ex-wife of a murderous drug dealer. But although the title suggests a family-friendly Schwarzenegger, the actual movie is not the broad farce the poster and trailers promise; in fact, it's barely a comedy at all. With its scenes of gun violence and upsetting toddler-in-peril climax, it's hardly appropriate fare for smaller children, but there's not much here for adults to enjoy, either, unless the fact that Schwarzenegger's unorthodox classroom methods end up working comes as some sort of revelation.

The Quotable Arnold: "It's not a tumor!"

16. *End of Days* (1999)—Schwarzenegger gives another of his late-period depressive performances in this preposterous supernatural thriller directed by Peter Hyams (*2010*, *Timecop*). Here he's an alcoholic, suicidal ex-cop who somehow gets mixed up in a biblical scenario that resembles a straight-to-DVD cross between *Seven* and *Rosemary's Baby*. Playing off our timeless fears of Y2K, *End of Days* posits a scenario in which the devil takes human form (Gabriel Byrne's human form, in fact) in the waning days of the twentieth century. With the help of a satanic cult, Old Scratch will open the gates of hell and bring about the apocalypse by . . . having sex with Robin Tunney between 11:00 p.m. and midnight on December 31, 1999. Seriously, that's the plan. (At least Arnold has the presence of mind to ask, "Is that Eastern Time?") The battle of Schwarzenegger vs. Satan sounds like a blast, but Hyams goes for solemn and ponderous instead, with turgid results.

The Quotable Arnold: "Between your faith and my Glock nine millimeter, I'll take the Glock."

15. *Raw Deal* (1986)—It's a promising set-up, at least: Drummed out of the FBI under shady circumstances and exiled to life as a small-town sheriff, Arnold gets the opportunity to earn back his badge by slicking back his hair, putting on a suit, and infiltrating the Chicago mob. As directed by John Irvin (*Hamburger Hill*), however, this is easily the dullest effort from Schwarzenegger's '80s heyday. The villains are smaller-than-life, the mob machinations wouldn't pass muster on an episode of *Miami Vice*, and the whole enterprise feels shoddy and low-rent. Worst of all is the star's smug, unlikable performance, which shades his acts of violence with an unpleasant, sadistic tinge. His final killing spree may not boast the highest body count in the Schwarzenegger ouevre, but given the context, it's certainly the most repellent.

The Quotable Arnold: "You should not drink and bake."

14. *Conan the Destroyer* (1984)—Superficially, at least, this sequel resembles a return to the world established in *Conan the Barbarian*: There's Arnold in his wig and loincloth, swinging a sword through some of the same locations, accompanied by the swelling Basil Poledouris score. But unlike the fevered John Milius original, this *Conan* has no madness to its method. Milius is gone, replaced by Richard Fleischer (*Fantastic Voyage*, *Soylent Green*), an old pro with no particular passion for the material. In hopes of turning Conan into a long-running, family-friendly franchise, the savagery of the original is all but absent, replaced by an emphasis on fantasy and comedy relief. The supporting cast appears to have been assembled by drawing names from a hat; Wilt Chamberlain, Grace Jones, and Tracey Walter are all out of place (and knowing what we know now, the notion of Chamberlain protecting the virginity of nubile Olivia d'Abo is ill-advised at best). This is a neutered Conan, punching horses and camels in the nose rather than decapitating his enemies without a second thought. It doesn't work, and the hoped-for franchise never materialized.

The Trivial Arnold: Milius had envisioned a trilogy of Conan adventures, but after he and Dino de Laurentiis had a falling-out, he was replaced as director of the sequel. As late as 2010, Milius hoped to film his script of *King Conan* with Schwarzenegger, but after the unsuccessful reboot of the series in 2011 (without the participation of either party), that would seem to be a long shot.

13. *The 6th Day* (2000)—Visions of the near future are always difficult to pull off. If you guess wrong more often than not, your film may end up looking more dated than a '70s roller-disco picture in just a few short years. Such is the fate of *The 6th Day*, a sci-fi thriller that takes place "sooner than you think" but gets the future embarrassingly wrong from the very first scene, set at an XFL football game. (The XFL, if you've forgotten, was an "X-treme" alternative to the NFL masterminded by wrestling mogul Vince McMahon. It lasted all of one season in 2001.) The title is a reference to the Book of Genesis, specifically the part about God creating man in his own image on the sixth day. In the world of sooner-than-you-think, human cloning has been banned, but that hasn't stopped Replacement Technologies mogul Tony Goldwyn and his top scientist, Robert Duvall, from pursuing it anyway. Schwarzenegger is a charter helicopter pilot who returns home from a flight with Goldwyn only to find another copy of himself at home with his wife and family. A *Philip K. Dick for Dummies* take on questions of identity and what it means to be human ensues, but the hoped-for Arnold vs. Arnold showdown never really materializes, and the protracted finale is a chore to endure.

The Quotable Arnold: "I might be back."

12. *Last Action Hero* (1993)—A punch line months before it was even released in the summer of 1993, and a notorious bomb when it finally arrived in theaters, *Last Action Hero* hasn't exactly aged into a underappreciated lost classic . . . but it has its moments. Conceived by original screenwriters Zak Penn and Adam Leff as a parody of the '80s-style action pictures Schwarzenegger and his counterparts rode to fame, *Hero* was brought to the screen by two of the very people who were being satirized, director John McTiernan (*Die Hard*) and screenwriter Shane Black (*The Last Boy Scout*), with predictably schizophrenic results. The central conceit dates back as far as Buster Keaton's *Sherlock, Jr.*: Danny, a young, fatherless boy, uses a magic ticket to enter the movie world of his favorite action hero, Jack Slater, where police stations resemble luxury hotel lobbies, cartoon cats solve crimes, and every cop is two days from retirement. Arnold has fun spoofing his image as a cigar-chomping loose cannon of a cop who speaks entirely in one-liners, but *Hero* ultimately falls flat, mainly because Danny's supposedly gritty reality proves to be just as artificial as the action-movie world Slater inhabits.

The Trivial Arnold: Among the movie's many in-jokes is a scene set in a video store within the Jack Slater movie world, featuring a stand-up display for *The Terminator* starring . . . Sylvester Stallone. Ah, what could have been.

11. *Red Heat* (1988)—Sam Peckinpah disciple Walter Hill made a name for himself in the '70s and early '80s with a series of stripped-down, kinetic action pictures (including *The Driver*, *The Warriors*, and *Southern Comfort*), but his biggest success came with the culture-clash, buddy-cop action-comedy *48 Hrs.* Hill returned to that formula with this glasnost-era thriller, but the volatile chemistry between Nick Nolte and Eddie Murphy was not so easily replicated. Schwarzenegger stars as a no-nonsense Moscow police officer who must team with James Belushi's slovenly, obnoxious Chicago detective to track down a Russian drug dealer now operating in the United States. Schwarzenegger's Ivan Danko is essentially the Terminator with a Vanilla Ice brush cut and a Russian accent: impassive, humorless, unstoppable. The contrast between his Soviet-style pragmatism and Belushi's usual loudmouth boorishness is only sporadically amusing, and Hill takes the standard-issue narco-terrorism plotline too seriously, peppering it with over-the-top gun violence. The movie's best joke is its casting of Reaganite American Dreamer Schwarzenegger as the embodiment of Iron Curtain austerity; when he turns on the TV in his hotel room only to find a porn movie in progress, he manages to sneer, "Capitalism!" with a straight face.

The Quotable Arnold: "I am not shitting on you."

10. *Running with Arnold* (2006)—The one movie least likely to be listed on Schwarzenegger's résumé, this muckraking documentary by first-time (and so far only-time) director Dan Cox casts a jaundiced eye at the actor's most controversial role: the Governator. As early as the mid-'70s, Arnold had been telling friends he would be governor of California one day, but it was not until 2003 that the opportunity presented itself, in the form of a recall election aimed at ousting the aptly named Gray Davis. The recall quickly became a freak show, with porn stars and aging sitcom has-beens throwing their names in the ring, but Schwarzenegger was able to separate himself from the pack with the backing of prominent Republicans. Cox's film is at its best when it focuses on Schwarzenegger's slick, substance-free campaign tactics and the candid moments when the candidate's smiling mask slips to reveal the gargoyle beneath. But it overreaches in its attempts to tie Schwarzenegger to a neo-Nazi ideology, as sardonic narrator Alec Baldwin noted when he petitioned to have his name removed from the documentary.

The Quotable Arnold *(to Arianna Huffington in a debate)*: "I just realized I have the perfect part for you in *Terminator 4*."

9. *Eraser* (1996)—This slick, paint-by-numbers thriller earns no points for originality, but its Looney Tunes execution of several action set-pieces makes it one of Schwarzenegger's more enjoyable post-'80s outings. A U.S. marshal with an extreme approach to witness relocation, the "Eraser" is tasked with protecting whistleblower Vanessa Williams, who has evidence that the defense contractor she works for is planning to sell a new high-tech weapon on the black market. (The gun fires an electromagnetic pulse at the speed of light—a pulse Schwarzenegger has no trouble dodging later in the movie.) Highlights include a sequence in which Arnold is nearly sucked into a plane's jet engine before managing to plummet fast enough to catch up with a parachute he'd accidentally dropped, and a battle with giant crocodiles featuring the finest CGI that 1996 had to offer.

The Quotable Arnold *(To a crocodile he's killed)*: "You're luggage."

8. *The Running Man* (1987)—Adroitly anticipating the reality-television craze, Paul Michael "Starsky" Glaser's prescient sci-fi thriller is like a special two-hour edition of *Fear Factor* featuring guest stars from *WWE Smackdown*. Schwarzenegger plays an ex-cop who has been framed for the mass slaughter of innocent civilians. His sentence: to appear on America's number-one game show, *The Running Man*. Released into a game zone covering forty city blocks, he and his cronies must evade the Stalkers—comic book executioners with names like Buzzsaw and SubZero—in order to escape with their freedom and fabulous prizes. Despite a modicum of wit in script and concept, *The Running Man* really only makes sense if you take it on faith that America in the year 2017 will be caught up in an all-consuming frenzy of 1980s nostalgia. Every element of the movie, from the score to the production design to the costumes and hairstyles, is absolutely state-of-the-art, assuming Ronald Reagan is still the president and Max Headroom is still the cutting edge of pop culture. It's easy to picture Glaser standing just out of camera range in his white *Miami Vice* suit and poofy mullet, urging the effects department to pump up the dry ice. And what a cast! Yaphet Kotto, Maria Conchita Alonso, Jim Brown, Mick Fleetwood, Dweezil Zappa, Richard Dawson, and Jesse Ventura—it's like the dream lineup for the next edition of *Dancing with the Stars*.

The Quotable Arnold: "I'm not into politics."

7. *Total Recall* (1990)—There's a great brain-teaser of a movie to be mined from the Philip K. Dick short story "We Can Remember It for You Wholesale," all about implanted memories and shifting levels of reality. *Total Recall* is not that movie, although it might have been. At one time, David Cronenberg was slated to adapt the story as a film, which no doubt would have been very different from the Paul Verhoeven spectacle that finally emerged from a long and tortured development process. That's not to say Verhoeven's take isn't entertaining in its own right, but this ultraviolent live-action cartoon decidedly emphasizes mayhem and special effects over the mind-bending aspects of Dick's work. The casting of Schwarzenegger as a blue-collar everyman is our first clue that everything is not what it seems; when his Doug Quaid visits a virtual travel agency to have false memories of a Martian vacation implanted in his brain, he discovers he's actually a secret agent named Hauser bent on taking down the corrupt corporate rulers of Mars. Or is he? You probably won't care by the time *Total Recall* rolls around to its preposterous climax, but with its gaudy visuals (featuring some of the last large-scale special-effects work of the pre-digital era), Rob Bottin's grotesque mutant makeup, and a body count numbering in the dozens, Verhoeven's film remains one of the guilty pleasures of its era.

The Quotable Arnold: "Consider that a divorce."

6. *Predator* (1987)—It's probably not possible to contract testosterone poisoning simply by touching a *Predator* DVD, but you might want to wear gloves anyway. As directed by John McTiernan, this manly-man action flick is awash in sweaty machismo from start to finish. Schwarzenegger leads a special-forces team summoned to perform a rescue mission in a dense Central American rainforest. It soon becomes clear that they've been sent under false pretenses, and that their true enemy is much more fearsome than the guerrilla forces they easily dispatch. Basically, it's *Alien* in the jungle, as Arnold and his formidable team (including fellow future governor Jesse Ventura, Carl Weathers, and Bill Duke), all toting guns the size of Winnebagos, are picked off by a hulking, technologically advanced hunter from the stars. McTiernan keeps the suspense taut, the action brutal, and the one-liners vulgar, and the result is one of Schwarzenegger's most satisfying hard-action outings. Sequels and crossovers with the *Alien* series would follow, but the star would not.

The Quotable Arnold: "If it bleeds, we can kill it."

5. *Pumping Iron* (1977)—Meet the real-life Terminator. A star was born in this documentary about the world of competitive bodybuilding, as Arnold Schwarzenegger found the role of a lifetime: himself. The twenty-eight-year-old denizen of Gold's Gym in Venice Beach, California, was not the only bodybuilder profiled in this film by Robert Fiore and George Butler, but from the opening frames, he's the one with his eye on the main chance. Charismatic, arrogant, and completely full of shit, Arnold proves to be a master manipulator as he conducts psychological warfare on his chief competitor for the title of Mr. Olympia, gentle giant Lou Ferrigno. Pioneering techniques that would later serve as building blocks for the reality-TV genre, Fiore and Butler shape the rivalry storyline by setting up contrived situations and accentuating the contrast between Arnold's golden-god Muscle Beach lifestyle and Ferrigno's depressing workouts in a dank Brooklyn gym populated by Daniel Clowes characters. The bodybuilding subculture the film portrays may appear bizarre to outsiders, but the participants seem oblivious to both the freak-show aspect and the homoerotic component of their chosen sport. By the end, when Schwarzenegger has completely shattered Ferrigno's self-confidence and ensured himself another Mr. Olympia title, it's clear that he's already set his sights on greater fame. But it feels a little bit like he's sold his soul in the process.

The Quotable Arnold: "I was always dreaming about very powerful people, dictators and things like that. I was just always impressed by people who could be remembered for hundreds of years, or even, like Jesus, be for thousands of years remembered."

4. *True Lies* (1994)—Schwarzenegger's post-Terminator reunion with James Cameron will be discussed in depth in the next chapter. For now, suffice it to say that this comedic update of 007-style spy movies features several of the most exciting action sequences—and some of the most uncomfortable moments—of both its director's and its star's careers.

The Quotable Arnold *(channeling his inner Donald Trump as he fires a missile upon which a terrorist is hanging)*: "You're fired."

3. *Stay Hungry* (1976)—While researching this adaptation of a novel by Charles Gaines, director Bob Rafelson (*Five Easy Pieces*) spent time on the bodybuilding circuit of the mid-'70s, despairing of ever finding an actor to play the book's aspiring Mr. Universe character Joe Santo. One of Rafelson's new muscleman friends was confident the director had already found his man. "You can look all over the world, Bob," Arnold Schwarzenegger told him, "and you will sooner or later turn to me to play this part." That explains the somewhat dubious "Introducing Arnold Schwarzenegger" credit at the beginning of *Stay Hungry* (evidently, Arnold had left *Hercules in New York* off his résumé), a generally easygoing comedy of New South manners. Jeff Bridges is a scion of old-money Birmingham, going through the motions of a real estate career, who falls in with the colorful characters at the run-down gym he's supposed to buy out. Both his high-society friends and his new disreputable pals assume he's slumming, but he soon develops a genuine affection for receptionist Sally Field and bodybuilder Schwarzenegger, who gives perhaps the most human-scaled performance of his career. The film takes an unfortunate turn toward the bizarre near the end, but for the most part, it has a relaxed, unhurried charm rarely glimpsed in the rest of the Schwarzenegger filmography.

The Trivial Arnold: Schwarzenegger won a Golden Globe for Best Acting Debut in a Motion Picture, despite the minor detail that *Stay Hungry* was not his acting debut.

2. *Commando* (1985)—Gleefully over-the-top and ludicrous in almost every respect, *Commando* should probably be Exhibit A for anyone arguing that action movies were simply more fun in the '80s. Everything about it is jacked up to the extreme, from Arnold's physique to the mustache-twirling villain (*The Road Warrior*'s Vernon Wells, resplendent in a mesh vest and leather pants) to James Horner's cacophonous score, all squealing synths, dinky drum machines, screeching saxophones, and steel drums for that Caribbean flavor that has nothing to do with anything. The plot is standard-issue: Schwarzenegger's awesomely named John Matrix is a former special-forces officer who must go on one final mission when his young daughter is kidnapped by a former colleague. What matters here is the comic-book flair that director Mark Lester (*Class of 1984*) brings to the proceedings. By the time Schwarzenegger and reluctant sidekick Rae Dawn Chong drive a truck into an army surplus store and break into the back room where the rocket launchers are stored, *Commando* has reached pop-action nirvana.

The Quotable Arnold: "You're a funny guy, Sully. I like you. That's why I'm going to kill you last."

1. *Conan the Barbarian* (1982)—As subtle and understated a film as you'd expect from the combined talents of John Milius, Oliver Stone, Dino de Laurentiis, and Schwarzenegger, the first

Conan adventure is exactly the movie it should be: pulpy, bloody, and bombastic as hell. Schwarzenegger was born to play Robert E. Howard's Cimmerian warrior, who is just the sort of muscle-bound sword-and-sandals hero he worshipped as a child sneaking into Hercules movies in Austria. Conan also proved to be the ideal vehicle for co-writer/director Milius's obsessions with history, warfare, and Nietzschean philosophy, all of which are much more palatable in the context of a fantasy epic. Enslaved as a child following the murder of his parents, Conan spends years pushing the Wheel of Pain (not to be confused with the Tree of Woe, upon which he is later crucified) before earning his freedom and seeking vengeance on snake cult leader Thulsa Doom (James Earl Jones). As designed by Ron Cobb (*Alien*), the movie resembles a Frank Frazetta painting come to life, and the overpowering score by Basil Poledouris is the icing on a deliriously excessive cake.

The Quotable Arnold: "To crush your enemies, see them driven before you, and hear the lamentations of their women!"

THE FIVE WORST ARNOLD SCHWARZENEGGER MOVIES

5. *Hercules in New York* (1969)—Also known as *Hercules Goes Bananas*, Schwarzenegger's feature film debut could hardly have been less auspicious. Billed as Arnold Strong, the first-time actor played the title role of his dreams in this low-budget fish-out-of-water comedy, but his Hercules is a petulant demigod indeed. Bored with life on Mount Olympus, he defies his father Zeus and plunges to Earth, where he hitches a ride on a steamer ship bound for New York City. After wiping the deck with a few swabbies, Herc jumps ship, takes a taxi to Central Park, and stiffs the cabbie for the fare. That sets the tone for the rest of the movie, as Hercules behaves like a rude, entitled jerk everywhere he goes. In other words, he's not a fish out of water at all—just a typical New Yorker. Schwarzenegger is understandably chagrined by his feature debut, in which he performs such embarrassing feats as wrestling a man in a bear suit and making his man-boobs dance to a jaunty, *Zorba*-like bouzouki soundtrack. But the greatest indignity of all came in post-production, when Schwarzenegger's voice was overdubbed. Consequently, every time he opens his mouth, he speaks not with that familiar Austrian accent, but with the smooth, mellow tones of an AM radio newscaster. (A later DVD release restores his original vocal track.) If you have any lingering questions about why it took Schwarzenegger more than a decade to establish an acting career, *Hercules in New York* should clear up that mystery.

The Quotable Arnold: "You have strucked Hercules!"

4. *Junior* (1994)—The third time was definitely not the charm for the team of Reitman and Schwarzenegger, who reunited with *Twins* costar Danny DeVito for this soggy male-pregnancy comedy. Once again, the poster is the premise for this high-concept piece of film engineering: a mugging DeVito holding a stethoscope to a wide-eyed Arnold's baby bump, as beatific love interest Emma Thompson looks on. DeVito and Schwarzenegger play a pair of gynecologists who have developed an experimental new fertility drug. When their university cuts off their funding, they are unable to secure FDA approval to test Expectane on women, so Schwarzenegger's dour Dr. Hesse reluctantly agrees to serve as "guest host" to a fertilized egg while testing the drug. You might think some humor could be mined from the spectacle of a pregnant Arnold getting in touch with his feminine side, but instead Reitman strains for poignancy, which is hard to pull off when his super-sized star is wearing a pink nightgown.

The Quotable Arnold: "My nipples are very sensitive!"

3. *Red Sonja* (1985)—Schwarzenegger may get top billing, but he plays second fiddle to cheese Danish Brigitte Nielsen, who makes her motion-picture debut as the title character in this campy sword-and-sandals outing. Despite the fact that Red Sonja was introduced in Marvel's *Conan* comic books, our man Arnold is in fact playing an entirely different long-haired barbarian named Kalidor, who aids Sonja in a quest to defeat the evil queen who slaughtered her family. At this point in his career, perhaps the actor wanted to prove he could play a wide range of shaggy, steroidal swordsmen—in this case, one who wears pants. Or maybe he wanted, just this once, to do a movie in which he didn't have the silliest accent. An annoying child sidekick and a plastic-looking mechanical sea monster rank highly on *Red Sonja*'s list of crimes against cinema, but worst of all may be the icky-triumphant moment when Kalidor and Sonja kiss and it looks like Arnold Schwarzenegger is making out with an Arnold Schwarzenegger impersonator.

The Quotable Arnold *(not actually in the movie, but long after its release)*: "It's the worst film I have ever made. Now when my kids get out of line, they're sent to their room and forced to watch *Red Sonja* ten times. I never have too much trouble with them."

2. *Jingle All the Way* (1996)—Every negative aspect of the holiday season is distilled down to ninety minutes in this woeful family comedy. Loud, crass, garish, alternately cynical and sentimental, *Jingle All the Way* might possibly entertain a sugar-rushing six-year-old with ADD, but everyone else would be better off nestled all snug in their beds. An absurdly miscast Schwarzenegger plays a workaholic suburban dad who neglects his son's Christmas-present request until the last minute, an oversight that proves disastrous when it turns out that the coveted Turbo Man action figure has been sold out for weeks. Sinbad brings his blustery brand of louder-is-better comedy to the proceedings as a rival dad, while the late Phil Hartman is wasted as a neighbor with an eye for Schwarzenegger's wife (Rita Wilson). Schwarzenegger desperately mugs his way through a role seemingly tailor-made for Steve Martin in his bland *Father of the Bride* mode; the result is about as much fun as being trapped in a mall full of screaming babies on Christmas Eve.

The Trivial Arnold: Schwarzenegger's *Red Heat* co-star James Belushi makes a cameo appearance as a department-store Santa in *Jingle All the Way*.

1. *Batman & Robin* (1997)—No matter how many awards he may win, or magazine covers he adorns, or starlets he beds, or good causes he spearheads, no one will ever let George Clooney forget he once wore the Batsuit with the nipples. And that's as it should be. It's astounding to think Arnold Schwarzenegger was able to overcome the scandalous footage of himself in full Mr. Freeze drag, willingly uttering lines like "Da ice man cometh!" and still be elected governor of California. And while it's nice that Joel Schumacher was finally able to achieve his lifelong dream of directing the Ice Capades, maybe someone should have pulled him aside and explained that this was actually supposed to be a Batman movie. Scientists have been unable to pinpoint with any exactitude the lowest moment of the Bat-franchise. Was it Robin surfing through the air, howling, "Cowabunga!" or the close-up of Clooney's bat-buttocks as he fastens his utility belt, or Schwarzenegger leading his minions in a chorus of "He's Mr. Snow-Miser"? To answer the question definitively would entail sitting through the entire movie again, and so far no one has been willing to take on the challenge.

The Quotable Arnold: "Ice to see you!"

THE OTHER '80S ACTION HERO: SYLVESTER STALLONE

Arnold Schwarzenegger's emergence as a star in the mid-1980s was accompanied by a new wave of pumped-up action heroes that included Chuck Norris, Jean-Claude Van Damme, and Steven Seagal. But Schwarzenegger's only serious competition for the top of the A-list was Sylvester Stallone. Stallone had envisioned a very different career for himself when he penned the original *Rocky* in the mid-'70s, insisting that he be cast in the lead role as a condition of selling the script. After *Rocky* won the Academy Award for Best Picture, Stallone was hailed as the new Brando in some quarters, but his subsequent working-class efforts like *F.I.S.T.* and *Paradise Alley* failed to find an audience. It seemed his fans only wanted more Rocky, and Stallone obliged.

In 1982, Stallone transformed his career with a pair of films that would establish him as an action icon. It was no surprise that *Rocky III* became a hit in the summer of that year, but the more cartoonish style of the film (which pitted Rocky against Mr. T's ferocious Clubber Lang) was a sign of things to come. That fall, Stallone played disillusioned Vietnam vet John Rambo in *First Blood*, a movie that had more in common with the antihero vigilante films of the '70s than the action spectacles to follow. Still, *First Blood* became an unexpected box office success, ensuring Rambo would return.

Unlike Schwarzenegger, who never took a creative hand in his action pictures, Stallone was almost always involved with the writing of his films, which took on an increasingly jingoistic tone as the Reagan era of "morning in America" unfolded. After the misfire of *Rhinestone*, an ill-advised musical pairing with Dolly Parton, Stallone enlisted both of his franchise characters in the Cold War. The 1985 summer blockbuster *Rambo: First Blood Part II* had originally been scripted by James Cameron, who disavowed the political content of the final product after Stallone rewrote his draft. As summed up by Rambo's line "Do we get to win this time?" the film re-fought the Vietnam War via a right-wing fantasy of POW rescue by a one-man American army. Politics aside, it was a rousing, crudely effective revenge picture, and it made Rambo a household name (even in the White House). The holiday-season hit *Rocky IV* pressed the pug from Philly into service in the fight against communism, as Rocky took on the Soviet-engineered fighting machine Ivan Drago. The quintessence of MTV-era filmmaking, *Rocky IV* consisted almost entirely of montages set to would-be hits from the soundtrack album.

Stallone's reactionary tendencies reached their fascist nadir with 1986's *Cobra*, in which he portrayed a steroidal caricature of a Constitution-shredding cop à la Dirty Harry. Despite his memorable "crime is a disease and I'm the cure" catchphrase, however, this character didn't catch on with American audiences, so Stallone dutifully retied his bandanna for 1988's *Rambo III*. Unwittingly revealing the pitfalls in using real-life geopolitics as a basis for action-adventure filmmaking, this third outing found Rambo battling Soviet troops alongside the Mujahideen in Afghanistan. Stallone's timing was off, as the Iron Curtain was about to fall, but *Rambo III* looks even worse today, when viewers can't help but wonder if Osama bin Laden was among those "freedom fighters" glorified by the movie. In any case, it soon became clear that Stallone had peaked as an action star, as the failure of 1989's arm-wrestling epic *Over the Top* demonstrated.

While Schwarzenegger's reign continued well into the '90s, Stallone struggled to remain relevant with limp comedies like *Stop! Or My Mom Will Shoot* and lame action flicks like *Judge Dredd*. The rivalry between the two actors, which had turned nasty at times (particularly when Schwarzenegger dismissed Stallone as a flag-waving phony in a 1985 interview), faded away as they teamed, along with Bruce Willis, on the Planet Hollywood restaurant chain. In 2010, they shared the screen for the first time in *The Expendables*, a throwback to the '80s-style action pictures that had made them famous in the first place. As it turned out, Planet Hollywood was big enough for both of them.

James Cameron on the set of *T2*. (TriStar Pictures/Photofest)

7

KING OF THE WORLD: JAMES CAMERON'S REIGN

A CURIOUS BOY

In a talk given at the TED Conference in February 2010, James Cameron described his childhood. "In high school, I took a bus to school, an hour each way, and I was always absorbed in a science-fiction book, which took my mind to other worlds and satisfied, in a narrative form, this insatiable sense of curiosity I had . . . And my love of science fiction actually seemed to be mirrored in the world around me, because this was the late '60s, and we were going to the moon, we were exploring the deep oceans, Jacques Cousteau was coming into our living rooms with his amazing specials . . . the Jacques Cousteau shows got me excited about the fact that there was an alien world right here on earth. I might not really go to an alien world on a spaceship someday, but that was a world I could really go to right here on earth."

The image of Cameron as a curious lad with his nose buried in a book or his eyes enraptured by an undersea special might not resonate with our conception of him as the micromanaging terror of movie sets and egomaniacal wielder of Academy Awards, but it's clear that the seeds of his career were planted at an early age. Raised in Chippewa, Ontario, Canada, by mother Becky, an artist, and father Phillip, an electrical engineer, Cameron had little inkling he'd one day be able to channel his creative impulses into a movie career. That all changed when he was seventeen years old and his father was transferred to a new job in Orange County, California.

After his senior year of high school, Cameron enrolled in Fullerton College to pursue a science degree, but his study time was spent at the library of nearby USC, already well known for launching the careers of such filmmakers as John Carpenter, John Milius, and George Lucas. After absorbing every aspect of the movie-making process he could glean from books, Cameron was ready for a more practical apprenticeship. He'd never get into USC, but the Roger Corman school of filmmaking was always open to anyone willing to work long, hard hours for little or no money.

Following in the footsteps of Martin Scorsese, Francis Ford Coppola, Jonathan Demme, and many others, Cameron got his foot in the door of the motion-picture industry by talking his way into an entry-level position on one of Corman's low-budget exploitation films. As Cameron later said in a *Premiere* magazine interview, "I figured I would get in there and spread like a virus. It was the best possible place for me." His first gig involved building models for Corman's 1980 *Star Wars/Magnificent Seven* mash-up, *Battle Beyond the Stars*. Written by yet another future filmmaker, John Sayles, and starring Richard "John-Boy" Thomas, Robert Vaughn, and John Saxon, *Battle* is laughable in many ways, but the model work is actually decent. And true to his word, Cameron didn't stop there.

"Jim functioned as model builder, effects cameraman, and art director all on the same shoot," Roger Corman recalls in his entertaining memoir *How I Made a Hundred Movies in Hollywood and Never Lost a Dime*. "He concocted his own powders, blew up his own models, and designed the pyro effects for a spectacular climax—demolishing Sador's spaceship—at our Venice studio in the middle of the night . . . In fact, Jim later said after doing *Terminator* that all he did was 'take everything we did on *Battle* and just do it all bigger.'"

Cameron immediately followed up his work on *Battle* with a visual-effects and matte-painting gig on John Carpenter's *Escape from New York*. Although this was not a Corman production, Cameron was able to underbid all the major effects houses in Hollywood and use Corman's New World facilities to design, build, and photograph several of *Escape*'s major set pieces. Carpenter's lo-fi post-apocalyptic vision surely stuck with Cameron when the time came to direct *The Terminator*. No sooner had he finished work on *Escape* than he was back at New World for Corman's latest Grade Z space opera, *Galaxy of Terror*. While *Battle Beyond the Stars* strained for a *Star Wars* vibe, *Galaxy* was a blatant ripoff of Ridley Scott's *Alien* . . . and thus an odd bit of foreshadowing in regard to Cameron's future career, although he couldn't have known it at the time. Cameron served as production designer for the film and eventually pushed his way into the role of second-unit director. Clearly already chafing at having so little control over the way his work would appear on film, Cameron was ready to direct.

THE FINEST FLYING-PIRANHA MOVIE EVER MADE

That opportunity came courtesy of two Italian producers who had acquired the sequel rights to Corman's *Piranha*, a B-movie take-off on *Jaws* directed with wit and verve by Joe Dante. After the producers happened to observe Cameron getting convincing performances from a bunch of maggots with the help of an electric current, they decided he was the man to direct their flying-fish epic *Piranha Part Two: The Spawning*. In truth, the Italians were contractually obligated to hire an American director under the terms of their deal with Warner Bros. Once the production got underway, they planned to fire Cameron and finish the movie without him.

That's exactly what happened twelve days into the Jamaica-based production, leaving Cameron, who'd gone to the bother of learning Italian in order to communicate with the crew, furious. Later, fearing the movie would destroy his reputation before he even had the chance to establish one, the nearly broke Cameron flew to Rome, where the picture was being edited. Cameron would sneak into the editing room at night to recut the footage, but eventually he was caught, leaving the final edit to lesser talents. (He did manage to convince Warner Bros. to let him reedit the American release of the movie.) To this day, Cameron disowns *Piranha Part Two*, insisting that *The Terminator* was his "real" first film, although he did tell James Lipton on *Inside the Actor's Studio* that it was "the finest flying-piranha movie ever made."

That's hard to dispute, but Leonard Maltin also had a point when he wrote, "You would have to have been psychic to have spotted any talent from James Cameron in this picture." Just as the first *Piranha* ripped off *Jaws*, the second takes its cues from *Jaws 2*, right from the opening deep-sea-diving sequence. It's amusing that this scene, in which a pair of divers explore the wreckage of a navy vessel, anticipates so much of Cameron's later work, but it's even more amusing when the divers remove their wetsuits in order to get busy in the sunken ship. Their soggy coitus is cut short when the divers are cut to pieces by the teeth of dozens of piranhas nesting in the wreck of the *Dwight Fitzgerald*.

As we later learn, these are no ordinary piranhas. They're killer super-fish, the result of a government experiment in genetic splicing gone haywire. We get our first glimpse of just how different these fish are when one of them emerges from a diver's corpse, à la the *Alien* chest-burster, and attacks a nurse at the morgue. It's an effective jump-out-of-your-seat moment, but alas, such shockers are scarce in a movie that spends much of its running time dwelling on the wacky antics at its Caribbean resort setting. As much as Cameron may have wanted to distance himself from the finished product, however, at least two good things came out of his *Piranha* experience, as far as his future career was concerned. He met Lance Henriksen, an actor who would play roles in several of his future projects. And he had a fever dream in Rome about a legless cyborg dragging itself across a floor toward its intended prey.

ALIENS AND *THE ABYSS*

While waiting for his star Arnold Schwarzenegger to discharge his obligations to *Conan the Destroyer*, James Cameron killed time before the start of his *Terminator* shoot by completing two screenwriting assignments, both sequels. The first was a follow-up to the 1982 Sylvester Stallone hit *First Blood*, in which the star played a troubled Vietnam vet named Rambo. Cameron had no involvement with the resulting film beyond his draft of the script, which underwent considerable revision by its star before reaching the screen in 1985's *Rambo: First Blood, Part II.* As Cameron told the *New York Times* at the time of the film's release, "The action is mine, the politics is Stallone's."

The second assignment proved considerably more interesting to Cameron. Producers Walter Hill and David Giler had convinced 20th Century Fox to pursue a sequel to Ridley Scott's *Alien*, despite the studio's reluctance. Having read the *Terminator* script, they decided Cameron would be a perfect fit for the project. Cameron was a fan of the original but had little interest in duplicating what Scott had done. Despite its science-fiction trappings—the outer-space setting, the titular alien—Scott's film had the structure and tone of a horror movie. Cameron felt that *Alien* fans were so rabid that "to do a clone of it, to take one small baby step away, would not do." Instead, he decided to take elements of the first movie and add "something I've always wanted to see realized, which is the idea of the military in the future." Thus Cameron's screenplay recast the sequel as a combat picture, right down to the platoon of misfit grunts straight out of every old World War II movie.

The key to getting the sequel off the ground was convincing star Sigourney Weaver, who played Ripley, sole survivor of the original *Alien*, to sign on. Fortunately for Cameron, Weaver didn't read his script very carefully. As she confessed on the making-of documentary included on the *Aliens* DVD, Weaver has a tendency to skip over the stage directions, which in this case meant she didn't quite grasp how artillery-intensive the movie would turn out to be. An antigun activist, Weaver wasn't thrilled to learn she'd be spending so much of the *Aliens* shoot toting oversized weaponry around the set.

With Weaver aboard, the film needed a director, and with the box-office success of *Terminator*, Cameron clearly emerged as the man for the job. After filling out the cast with several of his regular players, including Bill Paxton, Michael Biehn, and Lance Henriksen, Cameron and his producer (and now wife) Gale Anne Hurd began production at London's Pinewood Studios, with a largely British crew. To say the director and the Brits were a mismatch would be an understatement; Cameron's workaholic nature didn't mesh well with the frequent tea breaks, and his perfectionist nature didn't go over well with Pinewood veterans, who regarded him as an upstart novice. It was more or less at this point that Cameron's dictatorial side (referred to by colleagues as "Mij," or Jim spelled backward) began to take over, a state of affairs that would only intensify on subsequent productions.

Its filming may not have been smooth sailing, but the reception that greeted *Aliens* upon its release catapulted Cameron onto the A-list. It was one of the blockbuster hits of the summer of 1986, received generally positive reviews, and even scored a Best Actress nomination for Weaver, a rarity for a genre film. Today *Aliens* is generally remembered as a relentlessly intense two-plus hours of nonstop action, but that's not really the case. As the movie opens, Ripley is discovered by a salvage ship after spending fifty-seven years in hypersleep following the events of the first film. Having misplaced a valuable piece of company property, the spaceship *Nostromo*, Ripley is brought up on charges by the board of the corporation she'd worked for six decades earlier.

Cameron's portrayal of the corporatization of outer space is made depressingly believable by the mundanity of these early scenes, a trick he no doubt picked up from his favorite movie, *2001*. (Unctuous comedian Paul Reiser is particularly well cast as the corporate spokesman Burke.) When Ripley warns the suits on the board that the planet they've colonized is infested with alien eggs, their bottom-line reaction is no different than that of a contemporary real estate firm being told they shouldn't build their multimillion-dollar housing development on a toxic waste dump. Of course, once Ripley is proven right and the colonists are attacked by aliens, her reward is to return to the scene of the crime along with a detachment of marines in order to wipe out the threat.

The marines generally conform to stereotypes dating back to the earliest World War II movies, except that, in keeping with Cameron's MO of playing with gender roles in an action context, the toughest, most macho solider of all is a woman, Vasquez (Cameron regular Jenette Goldstein), while the biggest whiner is a man (Bill Paxton, in perhaps his most grating performance). As would become a recurring theme for Cameron, the military finds itself in conflict with another institution, in this case the corporate interests represented by Reiser. (The marines would just as soon nuke the colony into oblivion, but Reiser demurs, noting the "substantial monetary value attached to the site.") In a bit of foreshadowing for *Terminator 2*, the onboard android (Lance Henriksen this time, in lieu of the original *Alien*'s Ian Holm) proves to be a hero rather than a villain, despite Ripley's initial mistrust.

The central relationship in *Aliens* is the mother/daughter bond that develops between Ripley and Newt, the orphaned child and sole survivor of the alien attack on the colony. The showdown that ensues once Ripley comes face-to-face with the queen alien thus becomes a battle of mother vs. mother (not a particularly subtle piece of subtext, granted, but Cameron has never been one to downplay his bumper-sticker themes). Despite her reluctance to handle guns onscreen, Weaver delivers one of the earliest, and still most believable, turns as a female action hero. The flurry of action that closes the movie is a bit on the mechanical side, but undeniably effective in that "digging your fingernails into your date's arm" way.

The enormous success of *Aliens* granted Cameron considerable leeway on his next project, and he would seize that opportunity with a vengeance. You could certainly make the case that *The Abyss* was a self-indulgent project: It was based on a short story Cameron had written in high school, its central relationship drew heavily on Cameron's crumbling marriage to Gale Anne Hurd, and its ambitious underwater sequences would allow him to realize his childhood Jacques Cousteau fantasies on a grand scale. Before production began, according to a 2009 *New Yorker* profile, Cameron made a vow to 20th Century Fox president Leonard Goldberg. "'I want you to know one thing—once we embark on this adventure and I start to make this movie, the only way you'll be able to stop me is to kill me."

It was that kind of production. Like *Apocalypse Now* and *Fitzcarraldo* before it, *The Abyss* was an insane endeavor seemingly overseen by a madman. Cameron rented a never-completed nuclear power plant owned by hixploitation auteur Earl Owensby and filled its containment vessel with 8 million gallons of water, then ordered an enormous tarp draped over it in order to blot out the sun. The actors took diving lessons before production, then spent upward of five hours a day in the tank, often waiting around for scheduled shots that never happened. Ed Harris nearly drowned while filming one grueling sequence, and Mary Elizabeth Mastrantonio fled the set in tears after repeatedly reshooting a scene in which her character is forcefully resuscitated. The crew took to wearing T-shirts with slogans like "The Abuse" and "Life's Abyss and Then You Dive."

The behind-the-scenes drama proved far more compelling than the finished film, which can best be described as an interesting failure. Pushing three hours in its "special edition" form, *The Abyss* concerns an American submarine that sinks after an encounter with an unknown vessel, and the rescue attempt mounted by a navy SEAL team in conjunction with a team of oil workers on an underwater drilling rig near the site of the accident. In the course of this mission, crew foreman Harris is forced to work with his estranged wife Mastrantonio, designer of the experimental drilling platform, as well as SEAL commander Michael Biehn, who suffers a break from reality brought on by high-pressure nervous syndrome. Harris and Mastrantonio are drawn back together as each suffers a near-death experience, and both are astounded to encounter alien life forms deep beneath the ocean's surface.

The Abyss certainly has its moments. Cameron's insistence on re-creating actual deep-ocean conditions as realistically as possible may have nearly killed his cast and crew, but there's a tangible quality to the action here that's missing from so many of today's digital epics (Cameron's included). The sequence in which Harris goes to great lengths to revive a seemingly drowned Mastrantonio is almost too harrowing to endure, yet it also feels like the most romantic gesture possible. The claustrophobic tension of the underwater sequences is heightened by the heavy-breathing effects on the soundtrack, another trick Cameron picked up from

2001: A Space Odyssey. It's a shame the story never manages to transcend its high school origins.

The version of *The Abyss* released in theaters in 1989 featured a head-scratcher of an ending in which it appears that aliens have come to Earth specifically to save Ed Harris's marriage. When the extended version finally saw the light of day, the additional footage revealed a mounting crisis between the United States and Soviet Union centered on the sunken submarine. In another plot twist seemingly lifted from *The Outer Limits* (by way of *2010*), the aliens threaten to wipe out humanity with gigantic tidal waves unless mankind can put aside its warlike ways. It's amazing that the studio agreed to release the movie without these tsunami effects, which would certainly be the centerpiece of any marketing campaign if *The Abyss* were made today. Instead, the special-effects buzz centered on the brief CGI sequence in which a tentacle of water manipulated by the aliens morphs into the faces of Harris and Mastrantonio. Cameron would make much more use of this revolutionary technique in his next picture. Given the disappointing box office of *The Abyss*, his follow-up would have to be a sure-fire hit. It was time to return Arnold Schwarzenegger's calls about doing a sequel to a little movie they'd made together called *The Terminator*.

TITANIC UNDERTAKINGS

After *Terminator 2*'s blockbuster success reestablished Cameron as a box-office golden boy, his initial impulse was to flex his creative muscles by tackling a smaller, more intimate film. This was to be *A Crowded Room*, based on the nonfiction book *The Minds of Billy Milligan*, about a serial rapist with multiple personality disorder. Cameron got as far as writing the script and casting John Cusack in the lead role before the project fell apart, leaving him with a hole in his schedule. Once again, Schwarzenegger came calling, this time with an idea to remake the little-seen French comedy *La Totale!*, about a dull bureaucrat leading a double life as a secret agent. Both Schwarzenegger and Cameron were fans of the James Bond films and felt this premise could be the ideal springboard for a modernized take on the spy genre.

As was becoming the norm for Cameron productions, the budget for *True Lies* approached the gross national product of a small Central American country. The director raised eyebrows with his casting of Tom Arnold, then best known as Roseanne Barr's slovenly ex-husband, in the role of Schwarzenegger's sidekick. In truth, Arnold is better suited to his role than the movie's star is to his; while it's easy enough to buy Schwarzenegger as a 007-style superspy, his Clark Kent–ish alter ego as a boring computer salesman is a bit of a stretch. Then again, realism isn't exactly high on the list of priorities for this action-comedy, which delivers several of Cameron's most accomplished set pieces, as well as some of the most unsavory moments in any Cameron film.

The tone is set right from the opening moments, which riff on the classic James Bond pre-credit sequences as Schwarzenegger emerges from a lake outside an opulent estate and strips off his diving suit to reveal the white tuxedo that will allow him to mingle with the guests at the exclusive party he's been assigned to infiltrate. As an agent for "Omega Sector," Schwarzenegger is tasked with bringing down the terrorist organization Crimson Jihad; as a husband and father, he is detached at best. Schwarzenegger's sitcom-ish domestic life with mousy wife Jamie Lee Curtis and rebellious daughter Eliza Dushku is disrupted when he begins to suspect Curtis of having an affair. The absurdity of a secret agent utilizing all the most sophisticated surveillance and tactical assets our tax dollars can buy to determine whether his wife is cheating on him is good for a few a laughs, but the humor curdles when he and Arnold kidnap Curtis, subject her to a hostile interrogation, then give her a "mission" to pose as a prostitute and plant a bug in a terrorist's hotel room. Although it's played for comedy, there's an unpleasant edge of humiliation to the scene in which the frumpy housewife does a striptease for her disguised husband, revealing the hot-bodied sex goddess within.

On the plus side of the ledger, *True Lies* offers some thrills to rival the best of the James Bond films. Successfully combining comedy with action requires a deft touch, and Cameron displays that in a chase sequence in which Schwarzenegger mounts a police horse to catch up to a motorcycle-riding baddie. His pursuit takes him into a hotel lobby, through the ballroom, kitchen, and parking garage, and finally up an elevator to the roof, where the horse finally rebels, refusing to attempt the jump to a pool on another rooftop. The grand finale, which finds Schwarzenegger behind the controls of a Harrier jet over downtown Miami, is a brilliantly staged and breathtaking piece of large-scale action filmmaking. And in a romantic gesture that's pure Cameron, Schwarzenegger and Curtis rekindle their marriage with a passionate kiss while the mushroom cloud of a nuclear explosion billows in the distance.

Speaking of grand romantic gestures, Cameron's next film would set a *Romeo and Juliet* love story against the backdrop of an Irwin Allen disaster movie, and set any number of records in the process. These days, of course, *Titanic* is the stuff of legend: It was the most expensive film ever made. It was the highest-grossing movie of all time. It was an Oscar juggernaut, winner of eleven Academy Awards including Best Picture and Best Director. At the time the project was announced, however, it was hard to believe any studio would agree to finance another James Cameron ocean adventure, or that any actors who had heard anything about the making of *The Abyss* would want to help him make it.

Reports from the set of *Titanic* resembled *Mad* magazine parodies of a James Cameron production. The director was hemorrhaging money by the millions and falling weeks behind schedule. He'd built an insanely expensive set, topping even the nuclear-containment tank from *The Abyss*, with a 7/8th-scale model of the *Titanic* that could be tilted and flooded. Like Ed Harris before her, star Kate Winslet claimed she'd nearly drowned during filming. The Hollywood trades sharpened their knives, certain that Cameron's film would be a disaster on the order of the real *Titanic*'s maiden voyage.

Not for the last time, Cameron disappointed those rooting for his failure. But while there's no disputing *Titanic*'s financial success, its artistic merit is still debatable. Certainly *Titanic* will go down as one of the great spectacles in Hollywood history; Cameron's seamless assemblage of sets, models, and digital effects to depict the sinking of the ship is masterful. Leonardo DiCaprio and Kate Winslet display undeniable chemistry as the star-crossed lovers Jack and Rose, but their performances are undermined by Cameron's tin-eared script. If these two characters had met on dry land, there's not a chance we'd care about their by-the-numbers love affair. Still, *Titanic* was beloved to the tune of $1.8 billion in worldwide grosses, and its Academy Award–winning director was now truly the king of the world. He could announce that his next project would be a four-hour, black-and-white Michael Dukakis biopic, and 20th Century Fox would gladly hand over a check for $200 million.

Fortunately for us all, that didn't happen. Instead, Cameron mostly disappeared from view for the next decade, occasionally surfacing with a new documentary of his latest deep-ocean expedition. But as soon as he announced that production had begun on his magnum opus *Avatar*, history began to repeat itself. Once again Cameron's budget had exceeded the national deficit. Once again the filmmaker was pushing the limits of special-effects technology, designing new 3D cameras and taking digital imagery and performance capture to the next level of photorealism. Once again, as the production stretched into its third year and its costs spiraled out of control, the pundits waited for him to fall on his face. And once again, it didn't happen.

That *Avatar* eventually overtook *Titanic* as the highest-grossing movie of all time is still something of a head-scratcher. *Titanic*'s mass appeal is easy to explain: it's a variation on a classic love story, set against a spectacular backdrop. In a way, so is *Avatar*, but the world Cameron has created here is far more alienating and seemingly less accessible to a general audience. The story isn't especially original: Wounded vet Sam Worthington has his consciousness installed within a genetically engineered body designed to resemble the native Na'vi of the moon Pandora. The objective is to gain the trust of the locals and work out a deal for the precious power source Unobtainium that lies beneath their village. As usual in Cameron pictures, the military has other ideas, and when they attempt to raze the village and take the Unobtainium by force, Worthington joins forces with Zoe Saldana and her fellow Na'vi to battle the imperialist forces. (As with *Terminator*, Cameron faced charges of plagiarism, as readers of both Poul Anderson's novella *Call Me Joe* and the Russian *Noon Universe* novel series reported many similarities to those works in *Avatar*.)

As usual, Cameron's pro-environmental and antiwar themes are painted on the broad side of a barn, and his villain, the military commander, is a cartoonish mustache-twirler. But while *Avatar* sports all the flaws common to the rest of the Cameron catalogue, it lacks the visceral, tactile quality of the great action sequences in his earlier films. Cameron's transition from hardware to software may have enabled him to create some eye-popping images (although immersing in the aquarium-like world of Pandora for nearly three hours starts to feel like being trapped in the world's most expensive screensaver), but his real talent was always more down-to-earth. The digital battles of *Avatar* lack the weight and presence of the *Terminator* chases or the *Abyss* dives or even Schwarzenegger's horse race through the *True Lies* hotel. There's no turning back for Cameron, who has contracted with Fox for two *Avatar* sequels, and it's clear by now that his audience will follow wherever he goes. But he was a lot more fun back when he had no choice but to create his brand of mayhem in the real world.

FIVE JAMES CAMERON ODDITIES

Undersea Documentaries—Cameron's childhood love of those Jacques Cousteau specials found its ultimate expression in a series of documentaries exploring the wonders of the deep. In 2002's *Expedition: Bismarck*, originally broadcast on the Discovery Channel, Cameron and his crew explore the wreckage of the sunken German battleship the director calls "the Death Star of its time." Cameron and Bill Paxton returned to *Titanic*'s resting place for *Ghosts of the Abyss* (2003), a large-format doc originally designed to be viewed in IMAX theaters but now available on DVD. Perhaps most impressive is 2005's *Aliens of the Deep*, another large-format effort utilizing technology undreamed of by Jacques Cousteau to explore ten deep-ocean sites in both the Atlantic and Pacific. Some of the bizarre creatures they find far beneath the ocean's surface resemble special effects from one of Cameron's sci-fi films (although sadly, there are no flying piranhas to be seen).

***Dark Angel* (2000–2002)**—Debuting between *Buffy the Vampire Slayer* and *Alias* on the timeline of "ass-kicking chick" TV shows, *Dark Angel* (co-created and co-produced by Cameron) starred Jessica Alba as a genetically engineered superwoman who escaped as a child from the compound of the biotech company that made her. Following the detonation of an electromagnetic pulse bomb in the atmosphere, the United States has devolved into a third-world country. Alba is living undercover in the Seattle of 2019, working as a bike messenger and spending her free time looking for the other eleven "transgenic" children who escaped from Manticore with her. Initially a success for the Fox network, the series was shifted from Tuesdays to the notorious dead zone of Friday nights for its second season, which increasingly resembled a low-rent *X-Men* knockoff. Cameron directed the series finale, "Freak Nation," a rather pedestrian hour of television that finds Alba and her fellow transgenics under siege from a mutant-hating mob. It was too little, too late, and *Dark Angel* was canceled after two seasons due to faltering ratings.

***Solaris* (2002)**—Cameron had long considered directing a remake of Andrei Tarkovsky's contemplative 1972 science-fiction film *Solaris*, and as Steven Soderbergh learned when he got the same idea, Cameron's Lightstorm Entertainment held the rights to both the original film and the novel by Stanislaw Lem on which it was based. Cameron agreed to produce with Soderbergh directing, but for all its potential, the resulting film is a humorless journey into a philosophical void. George Clooney stars as a psychologist summoned to investigate strange happenings on the space station orbiting the ocean planet Solaris. Upon arriving, he finds his recently deceased wife (Natascha McElhone) seemingly alive and well. Though Soderbergh clearly wants to wrestle with weighty issues of memory, identity, mortality, and loss, the script he's written doesn't come close to being up to the task. While the cinematography is impeccable (Soderbergh lenses under the pseudonym "Peter Andrews") and the set design convincing, the human element is sorely lacking, and the film ends up playing like a *Star Trek* episode directed by someone who's been reading up on Antonioni films in back issues of *Sight and Sound*.

***Sanctum* (2011)**—Cameron's screen credit may be limited to "Executive Producer," but his influence is all over this fact-based adventure film, which combines several of his pet obsessions: underwater action, computer-generated imagery, and 3D cinematography. Directed by Australian filmmaker Alister Grierson (*Kokoda*), *Sanctum* follows an exploration team deep into "the mother of all caves" in Papua New Guinea. When a major storm hits, their return route is blocked and they are forced to try to find another means of escape. Although it boasts several effective suspense sequences, including one in which two divers are forced to "buddy-breathe" through a flooded cavern, the film is less successful at depicting authentic human relationships. The literal-minded script forces its characters to voice every grudge, motivation, and bit of exposition in the most blunt, explicit terms, rather than allowing the conflicts to emerge organically from the story. What could have been a stripped-down, intense tale of survival is instead waterlogged with hackneyed daddy issues and implausible behavior.

Aquaman—Not an actual Cameron project, although it sounds plausible enough—which is probably why the makers of HBO's inside-show-biz comedy *Entourage* cast him as the director of their movie-within-the-show. After all, Cameron tried for years to adapt *Spider-Man* for the screen, only to be thwarted by rights issues, and although Aquaman has long been the punch line of the Justice League of America (how many crimes occur underwater, anyway?), his ocean kingdom would be right up the filmmaker's alley. Cameron gamely sent up his egomaniacal control-freak persona over the course of several episodes, but his insistence that the fake *Aquaman* movie be a hit within the fictional world of *Entourage* displayed the limits of his sense of humor.

KATHRYN BIGELOW

Perhaps more impressive than any of the large-scale productions James Cameron has overseen is the array of attractive, talented women he's been able to woo and wed. His early producer, Gale Anne Hurd, and two of his leading ladies, Linda Hamilton and Suzy Amis, are among those who said "I do" (and, except for Amis, "now I don't"), but perhaps the most accomplished of all Cameron's wives is director Kathryn Bigelow, to whom he was married from 1989 to 1991. Her box-office clout may not measure up to her ex-husband's, but her filmography is, in many ways, more varied and interesting. Here are five of her most notable efforts.

The Loveless (1982)—Bigelow co-wrote and co-directed her first feature with frequent David Lynch collaborator Monty Montgomery, so perhaps it shouldn't be surprising that *The Loveless* often resembles a collection of outtakes from a nonexistent Lynch film. Willem Dafoe makes his film acting debut as the leader of a 1950s motorcycle gang en route to the races in Daytona. Trouble begins to brew when the greasers make a pit stop in a small southern town, but it doesn't brew quickly. Dafoe and his gang (and by extension, the movie itself) are all about poses and attitude; looking and acting cool are all that matter to these punk nihilists, and narrative certainly takes a back seat to style for Bigelow and Montgomery, who linger over seemingly aimless scenes at diners and gas stations, leaving it to the vintage rock 'n' roll beat on the soundtrack to provide a steady pulse. But even though not much happens for the first hour or so, *The Loveless* does work its way under your skin as a mounting sense of unease builds to a startling, violent climax.

Near Dark (1987)—Bigelow's best film is your basic boy-meets-girl, girl-bites-boy, boy-develops-taste-for-blood story, but this violent, intense outing will never be mistaken for one of the *Twilight* movies. Bigelow and co-writer Eric Red had wanted to make a western, but in order to make the project more bankable, they had to disguise it as a horror movie. As *Near Dark* opens, we might be in Larry McMurtry country, all pickup trucks, quiet small-town streets, and lonely ol' nights. That's the landscape young farmhand Adrian Pasdar is itching to escape, and he gets the opportunity when he meets alluring Jenny Wright. Unfortunately, Wright comes as part of a package deal with her bloodthirsty "family" of fellow vampires, including three James Cameron regulars: Bill Paxton, Lance Henriksen, and Jenette Goldstein. Their dark ride through the American Midwest includes two showstopping set pieces: a bloody round of cocktails at a seedy roadhouse, and a showdown with the police at a roadside motel. Only at the end does *Near Dark* let up and deliver a perhaps too-happy resolution, but most of the way, it's a hell of a ride.

Point Break (1991)—Its release date may be 1991, but in many ways, *Point Break* feels like the last action movie of the '80s. Goofy and over-the-top, without getting bogged down in CGI, fireballs, and seizure-inducing editing, it's pre–Michael Bay action filmmaking at its most testosterone-poisoned . . . so naturally, it could only have been directed by Kathryn Bigelow. The role of quarterback-turned-FBI-agent Johnny Utah fit Keanu Reeves like the wetsuit he often sports in the movie, and only Patrick Swayze could have played the golden god Zen master of surfing and bank robbing, Bodhi. *Point Break* is basically a two-hour dick-measuring contest, which Reeves wins by jumping out of a plane without a parachute and using his sheer dudeness to fall faster than Swayze.

Strange Days (1995)—James Cameron produced and co-wrote this tech noir set on the last two days of 1999. Ralph Fiennes is a disgraced ex-cop who now makes his living dealing black-market virtual-reality clips, which allow "wire-tripping" users to relive moments from their own lives, or experience another person's memories. When Fiennes starts receiving envelopes containing snuff clips from the point of view of a psychotic rapist-murderer, he is drawn into a mystery that also involves his ex-girlfriend, aspiring rock star Juliette Lewis. The ambitious story, which also includes an incendiary subplot concerning the assassination of a famous rapper at the hands of the LAPD, never really coheres, and Bigelow gets a little carried away in her depiction of near-future Los Angeles as an urban hellscape (the crew appears to have standing orders to set something on fire in every scene), but if *Strange Days* is a failure, it's at least an honorable one.

The Hurt Locker (2009)—If living well is the best revenge, triumphing over your ex-husband at the Oscars must be a close second. That's what happened at the Eighty-second Academy Awards, when Bigelow's Iraq War–set thriller took the top prize and netted her Best Director honors over *Avatar* nominee Cameron. Less a commentary on the specifics of the Iraq conflict than a tense, jittery exploration of an adrenaline junkie's mindset, *The Hurt Locker* offers several nail-biting suspense sequences to rival anything in Cameron's filmography.

The Terminator comes to TV, with Lena Headey as Sarah Connor. (Fox Broadcasting/Photofest)

8

I'LL BE BACK: *THE TERMINATOR* SEQUELS AND TV SERIES

TERMINATOR 2: JUDGMENT DAY

The seeds of a sequel were planted in two scenes that were deleted from the original *Terminator* before its release in theaters on October 26, 1984. Both scenes are included on the *Terminator* DVD, along with commentary from James Cameron explaining why he cut them. In "Sarah Fights Back," Sarah Connor looks up the address of Cyberdyne Systems, the tech company that will eventually build Skynet and the Terminators. She tries to convince Kyle Reese that if they blow up Cyberdyne headquarters, they can prevent the coming nuclear war from ever happening. Reese insists that's not his mission, they quarrel, and Sarah runs into the woods. Reese pursues her, nearly shoots her, then breaks down crying at the sight of the surrounding natural beauty he's been denied all his life in the bleak, post-apocalyptic future. Cameron deleted the scene because he felt this emotional moment undercut a later scene between Sarah and Reese, but its omission from the movie had an unintended consequence. "It's absolutely great luck for me that I cut that scene, because it became the nucleus of the entire second film," Cameron says on the commentary. "So it gave us a reason to continue the story, because there was that unfinished piece of business."

The other deleted scene, "The Factory," would have given the first film a *Twilight Zone*–ish twist ending, as it is revealed that the site of Sarah's final battle with the Terminator is, in fact, Cyberdyne Systems. When workers discover a mechanical arm and a computer chip that have survived the Terminator's destruction, the implication is clear that Cyberdyne's study of these remains will lead to the building of Skynet and the Terminators. (Cameron says he cut this scene because "the acting was really bad.") Had the scene remained, it no doubt would have been perceived as the setup for a sequel, but in fact, Cameron had no intention of making one. It would take years to persuade him otherwise.

Unlike Cameron, Arnold Schwarzenegger was keen to make a sequel to *The Terminator*, although he didn't want to do it with Hemdale, the production company that held the rights. Schwarzenegger envisioned *Terminator 2* as an epic spectacle, well beyond Hemdale's means, so he was thrilled when producers Mario Kassar and Andrew Vajna purchased the *Terminator* rights from Hemdale through their company Carolco Pictures. Now that money was no object (and indeed, with its $100 million budget, *Terminator 2* was the most expensive movie ever made at the time of its production), Cameron saw a way to revive an idea he'd had to abandon in the first film because it was not yet technically feasible: a shape-shifting, liquid metal Terminator. With the computer-generated pseudopod of *The Abyss* serving as proof of concept, Cameron was convinced that it was now possible to pull off the most ambitious use of digital effects yet attempted.

Cameron and co-writer William Wisher hashed out a story they jokingly referred to as "a boy and his Terminator." The sequel would pick up more than a decade after the original, with Sarah Connor in a mental ward and the now ten-year-old John Connor living with foster parents and getting into trouble. Cameron and Wisher toyed with the idea of casting Schwarzenegger as both the Terminator sent to kill young Connor and the protector sent by the future John Connor but in the end decided to make it a simple role reversal, with Schwarzenegger playing a T-800 model Terminator reprogrammed by the good guys. The actor resisted at first—what fun is a Terminator that doesn't kill anyone?—but eventually saw the wisdom of this creative decision. Robert Patrick, then a relative unknown, was cast as the shape-shifting T-1000, while thirteen-year-old Edward Furlong, who had never acted before, took on the role of young John Connor.

Schwarzenegger may have been the highest-paid actor and the driving force behind the film's production, but *Terminator 2: Judgment Day* belongs to Linda Hamilton, returning as a transformed Sarah Connor. Hamilton underwent an extensive training regimen before shooting began, emerging physically transformed into a lean, sinewy action heroine. But it is not only Sarah Connor's body that has changed as *T2* begins; she really does seem to have been driven half insane by her foreknowledge of the coming nuclear holocaust. Hamilton delivers a fierce, fearless performance, courting unlikability as she executes the plan that was excised from the original *Terminator*, first by attempting to assassinate Cyberdyne scientist Miles Dyson (Joe Morton), and finally by enlisting Dyson in the cause of destroying his life's work.

As a filmmaker, Cameron had undergone his own transformation, one diametrically opposed to that of his leading lady. Where the first *Terminator* was lean and mean, the sequel is sprawling and outsized (and even more so in its special-edition DVD cut, which runs nearly two hours and forty minutes). Although it might have been improved with a bit of fat trimming, *T2* is nonetheless the most bracing and structurally sound of Cameron's large-scale action epics. For once, the director's big-picture themes are inseparable from his storytelling, as the concept of fate versus free will is built into the time-travel plot right from the opening scene of an older, scarred John Connor observing a battle in the future War Against the Machines. The film's major action set pieces, including the chase through the L.A. River and the final battle with the T-1000 at the steel mill, are as thrilling as anything Cameron has done. The computer-generated imagery marked a turning point for Hollywood special effects, even in its most subtle usage, such as digitally erasing wires from stunt sequences. Schwarzenegger brings unexpected humor to his portrayal of a Terminator attempting to learn human behavior from an adolescent boy, and Patrick gives a witty physical performance as the sleeker model Terminator.

In the end, Cameron comes down on the side of free will, if not quite as definitively as he'd originally planned. *Terminator 2* now ends on the image of an open road that might lead anywhere, but a coda set in a revised 2029 where Skynet never took over and John Connor has become a U.S. senator was deleted before the film was released. (It can be seen on the various DVD releases or on YouTube.) That ending might have closed the door on any future *Terminator* projects, but even without it, Cameron felt he had told the complete story. In his mind, the Connors had changed the future and there was nothing left to say. The marketplace would dictate otherwise, but the *Terminator* saga would have to continue without Cameron's participation.

Cameron wasn't *quite* done with the franchise yet, however, as the director couldn't resist when Universal Studios approached him with the idea for a theme-park attraction based on the Terminator. Schwarzenegger, Hamilton, Furlong, and Patrick all joined Cameron for *T2 3-D: Battle Across Time*, a multifaceted interactive experience including a twelve-minute short film in which the T-800 and John Connor attack the Skynet base of the future after once again escaping the T-1000. It's not a particularly meaningful extension of the Terminator story, but its emphasis on overpowering 3D spectacle certainly points the way toward Cameron's filmmaking future.

TERMINATOR 3: RISE OF THE MACHINES

Despite its gargantuan budget, *Terminator 2* was a massive box-office success, earning over half a billion dollars in worldwide grosses. Such staggering numbers should have all but guaranteed another sequel, but several obstacles stood in the way. Cameron's reluctance to continue was a major one, but even that could have been overcome had he been able to secure the rights to the franchise when Carolco went bankrupt in the mid-1990s. "There's a factory somewhere in the future cranking these suckers out," Cameron told *Platinum* magazine in 1995, "so we could always go back to it if we wanted to." When Carolco's assets went up for auction, Cameron was outbid for the company's share of the *Terminator* rights by Andrew Vajna and Mario Kassar, who then turned around and purchased the remaining rights from Cameron's ex-wife Gale Anne Hurd. Cameron was so miffed, he bowed out of any future dealings with the Carolco founders, which left the producing pair with another problem: Schwarzenegger had vowed never to make a *Terminator* movie without Cameron.

Of course, actors always reserve the right to change their minds, particularly after a few failures on the order of *Jingle All the Way* and *End of Days*. In 2000, Schwarzenegger agreed to reprise the role for Vajna and Kassar under their new production banner, C2. *Tank Girl* screenwriter Tedi Sarafian was commissioned to write the screenplay, later rewritten by John Brancato and Michael Ferris. While Schwarzenegger still held out hope that Cameron would come aboard as director, it was Jonathan Mostow (*Breakdown*, *U-571*) behind the camera when production began on April 12, 2002.

Terminator 3: Rise of the Machines opens ten years after the events of its predecessor. The prophesied Judgment Day of August 29, 1997, has come and gone, Sarah Connor has died of leukemia, and John Connor (now played by Nick Stahl) is a man in his early twenties, living off the grid as a drifter. Although it seems he's escaped his fate to become the leader of the human resistance, he's still haunted by dreams of metal assassins with big guns. And rightfully so, as it turns out, because another new-and-improved killer cyborg from the future, the T-X Terminatrix (Kristanna Loken), has just arrived in a Beverly Hills shop window. Once again, a protector has also been sent through time by the resistance—a reprogrammed T-850 Terminator in the familiar 101 model (Arnold Schwarzenegger). This time, however, the vintage Terminator has orders to protect not only John Connor, but his future wife and second-in-command Kate Brewster (Claire Danes).

It's an unwritten rule of sequels that history repeats itself as self-parody, usually by the time a series reaches its third installment, and *Terminator 3* is no exception. After Schwarzenegger makes his naked arrival in *T3*, he gets his usual menacing outfit not from a punk, as in the first movie, or a biker, as in the second, but from a leather boy doing a striptease at Ladies' Night. (The capper on this gag comes when the Terminator reaches into his jacket for sunglasses and dons a pair of star-shaped Elton John shades circa 1975.) Schwarzenegger's one-liners are goofier than ever ("Talk to the hand!"), and there's a certain campiness to his performance in general, as if he hasn't quite shaken off his role as Mr. Freeze in *Batman & Robin*.

This parodic element is one reason many Terminator purists would like to pretend *T3* doesn't exist, but there's a larger one. While the two films directed by James Cameron conclude that "there is no fate but what we make," Mostow's sequel insists that "Judgment Day is inevitable." To its detractors, *Terminator 3* is a disrespectful refutation of everything the Cameron movies stand for; while the first two *Terminator* films say we have free will and control over our destinies, the third says we're screwed no matter what we do. Indeed, as we learn in its third act, *T3* takes place on Judgment Day, which was not averted in *T2*, but merely postponed. The film ends with John Connor and Kate Brewster locked away in a fallout shelter built to house the highest government officials, while the world ends around them.

Despite this grim finale, however, *Terminator 3* is actually good fun for most of its running time. It's certainly flawed as a follow-up to the story Cameron created (the brusque dismissal of the Sarah Connor character is another sticking point, as is Stahl's rather wimpy take on John Connor), but judged on its own merits, it delivers exactly the sort of slam-bang rollercoaster ride so many summer movies aspire, but fail, to achieve. The humor may be overly broad at times, but a less ponderous *Terminator* isn't such a bad thing, and the running gag about the T-850's obsolescence and decrepitude is a sly way of acknowledging that Schwarzenegger really is getting too old for this shit. The action sequences are nearly seamless blends of practical stunt work and cutting-edge CGI, particularly the epically destructive chase scene involving a gigantic crane truck. And the mythology of the Terminators and Skynet is expanded in an entertaining way (particularly in a deleted scene, available on the DVD, in which Schwarzenegger appears as the human model for the T-101 series, the southern-accented Sergeant Candy).

Terminator 3 wasn't quite as big a hit as its predecessor, but it still grossed nearly half a billion dollars worldwide, seemingly guaranteeing another sequel. But a scant few months after the film's release, in a twist more ludicrous than any Hollywood screenwriter could have concocted, its star became the governor of California. Could the *Terminator* franchise carry on without both James Cameron and Arnold Schwarzenegger?

TERMINATOR: THE SARAH CONNOR CHRONICLES

With their iconic star otherwise occupied, producers Andrew Vajna and Mario Kassar turned their attention to the small screen. In 2005, C2 Pictures, in conjunction with screenwriter Josh Friedman (2005's *War of the Worlds*), began to develop a television series based on the *Terminator* films. Friedman's concept had the series picking up several years after the events of *Terminator 2* and focusing on Sarah Connor. British actress Lena Headey (now best known for *Game of Thrones*) was cast as Sarah, while Thomas Dekker of *Heroes* won the role of teenage John Connor. The pilot episode, written by Friedman and directed by television vet David Nutter, was shot in 2006. Days before the series was picked up by the Fox network in 2007, C2 was dissolved and the *Terminator* rights were sold once again, this time to the Halcyon Company. (Vajna and Kassar remained on the series as producers.) Halcyon had been formed for the specific purpose of acquiring all rights to *Terminator*, and by the time *Terminator: The Sarah Connor Chronicles* premiered on January 13, 2008, a fourth movie was already in the works.

In a 2007 interview with IGN.com, Friedman spoke about the series' relationship with the movie franchise, specifically its seeming conflict with the events of *Terminator 3*. "I think the thing about *T3* is, obviously there was just no Sarah Connor and that's something the fans were never happy with . . . So I almost think of this as *T3*. To me it takes the place of *T3*. But also I think that sort of in the spirit of *Terminator*, it's an alternate timeline. I know a lot of people get very worked up about the continuity and the canon and all that stuff."

As the premiere episode of the series opens, it is 1999, and Sarah Connor is a fugitive on the FBI's Most Wanted list for her actions in destroying Cyberdyne (and, it is believed, killing Miles Dyson). While she and John are living under assumed names in

New Mexico, a Terminator posing as John's substitute teacher opens fire in the classroom. John is saved by his classmate Cameron (Summer Glau), a protector Terminator whose name serves as homage to the creator of all Terminators. (Unless you subscribe to the notion that Harlan Ellison is the creator of all Terminators, in which case Richard T. Jones is on hand as the Connors' pursuer, FBI Agent James Ellison.)

Cameron helps the Connors escape the Terminator known as Cromartie with the help of some handy time-displacement equipment that allows them to jump forward eight years to September 2007. The rest of the first season (originally intended to run thirteen episodes, but cut down to nine due to the Writers Guild strike) finds the Connors and Cameron posing as the Baum family in Los Angeles, evading Terminators, and trying to track down an artificial-intelligence prototype called The Turk that may one day become Skynet.

The premiere episode of what fans came to call *Terminator: TSCC*, airing in a cushy timeslot following an NFL playoff game, attracted over 18 million viewers. After moving to its regular Monday-night spot on the Fox schedule, its ratings dropped to an average of around 8 million viewers, still a strong enough performance to ensure the show's continuation. The twenty-two-episode second season debuted on September 8, 2008, and featured three new series regulars: Brian Austin Greene as Derek Reese, resistance fighter and brother of John's late father Kyle Reese; former Garbage lead singer Shirley Manson as Catherine Weaver, a shapeshifting T-1001 Terminator posing as the CEO of a tech firm with interest in The Turk; and Garret Dillahunt as first the Terminator Cromartie, and later John Henry, the personification of The Turk. Ratings for *Terminator: TSCC* dwindled over the course of the season, particularly once Fox pulled it from the schedule for two months and returned it in a Friday-night timeslot. When the final second-season episode aired in April 2009, the show's fate was still unresolved, as were its storylines.

As is the nature of the beast with network television, *Terminator: TSCC* has its ups and downs, but the thirty-one existing episodes (all available on DVD) are certainly worthy of investigation by any fan of the movies. (See the Top Five list at the end of this chapter for a rundown of the highlights.) The first season is the more consistent of the two, which is to be expected given its relative brevity, but the second season is more ambitious, if a bit too sprawling and unfocused at times. Lena Headey projects the toughness and fierce determination of Sarah Connor convincingly enough, but the madness isn't there, and by the second season her performance has calcified into dour surliness marked by an ever-present grimace. Thomas Dekker has brooding teen angst to spare as John Connor, but the best acting in the series comes courtesy of the supporting cast, most notably Glau and Dillahunt.

The robot that wants to be more human is one of sci-fi television's tiredest tropes (e.g., Data of *Star Trek: The Next Generation*), but Glau undercuts the sentimental pitfalls inherent in such a role with blunt insolence and deadpan humor. Dillahunt had played two different roles on a series before, portraying both Wild Bill Hickock's killer Jack McCall and George Hearst's emissary Francis Wolcott on the late, lamented *Deadwood*. Here he has the even trickier task of playing two machines, one single-minded and deadly, the other inquisitive and friendly, and delivers two distinct portrayals laced with mischievous wit. The game-changing ending of the second-season finale promised a whole new set of challenges for these actors, but on May 18, 2009, Fox officially canceled the series, only three days before the theatrical release of the fourth *Terminator* movie.

TERMINATOR SALVATION

Producers Kassar and Vajna had originally hoped to film *Terminator 3* and *4* in relatively rapid succession. When it became clear that Schwarzenegger's political career would scuttle any chance of his return, *T3* screenwriters John Brancato and Michael Ferris shifted gears, conceiving a scenario that worked around the star's absence. By 2005, preparations for the fourth film were far enough along that Nick Stahl would tell Sci-Fi Wire, "I'm not going to be in *T4*. None of the cast is coming back . . . I believe it's a jump to the future, so my character will be quite a bit older." The collapse of C2 following the failure of its abysmal *Basic Instinct 2* in 2006 threatened to delay *T4* until Judgment Day, but once Halcyon purchased the rights in 2007, the sequel was back on track.

Filming got underway in May 2008 with neither James Cameron nor Jonathan Mostow behind the camera. Instead, it was Joseph McGinty Nichol, the filmmaker always credited as "McG," in the director's seat. Best known for his frenetic, goofy *Charlie's Angels* movies, McG probably wasn't the first choice of any Terminator fan who hated the campy aspects of *T3*, but to be fair, he took the material very seriously. Perhaps *too* seriously, as the movie eventually released as *Terminator Salvation* is easily the grittiest, most humorless entry in the series. Unlike the first three movies, *Salvation* features no time travel and no contemporary setting; aside from a brief prologue set on the eve of Judgment Day, the entire film takes place in the year 2018, with the War Against the Machines in full swing. In the prologue, we learn that death-row inmate Marcus Wright (Sam Worthington) signed his body over to Cyberdyne Genetics for medical testing in 2003. Fifteen years later, Marcus awakens in a strange new world—gray, decimated, and crawling with murderous machines. Rescued from a T-600 attack by a teenage Kyle Reese (Anton Yelchin), who is later taken prisoner by Skynet, Marcus makes his way to the Los Angeles stronghold of the resistance. There he meets John Connor (Christian Bale), who discovers that Marcus is actually a cyborg who believes he is human. Despite their initial mistrust, Connor and Marcus team up to rescue Kyle from Skynet and destroy a major Terminator production line.

With its bleached imagery, grim tone, and near-continuous battle action, *Salvation* often feels more like a reboot of the *Mad Max* saga than a *Terminator* film. It may have been too much of a departure for many fans, and it didn't help that the pre-release buzz primarily centered on a recording of Christian Bale's profane rant at a crew member. Still, the movie is not without its strong points. The attack on a gas station by a sixty-foot Harvester robot suggests what Transformers might look like if they were actually scary, and John's encounter with an original 101 model T-800 (made possible by digitally scanning a mold of Schwarzenegger's head from 1984) is an unexpected treat. Overall, though, *Salvation* is far too monochromatic, both in look and tone, and Bale's why-so-serious performance is its dour match.

Despite largely negative reviews and audience reaction, *Terminator Salvation* still performed well, taking in nearly $400 million in worldwide grosses. Talk of the film being the first in a new *Terminator* trilogy was quickly shelved, however, as the Halcyon Company filed for bankruptcy protection against the hedge fund that had supplied its financing. By now, the franchise almost seemed cursed, as each *Terminator* film had been produced by a different company, all of which had gone out of business. At this point, the rights issues are every bit as tangled and convoluted as the Terminator timeline. But as we'll see in the Afterword, the franchise, like the unstoppable robots it centers on, refuses to die.

THE FIVE BEST EPISODES OF *TERMINATOR: THE SARAH CONNOR CHRONICLES*

"Queen's Gambit"—The series really hit its stride in this fifth episode, in which Sarah's potential love interest Andy enters his artificial-intelligence prototype, The Turk, in a chess tournament. If The Turk wins, increasing the odds that it will eventually become Skynet, Cameron will kill Andy. The Turk loses, but Andy is killed anyway, and Sarah and John are startled to learn that the assassin is not only from the future, but is John's uncle, Derek Reese.

"What He Beheld"—The first-season finale opens with a flash-forward scene of young Derek and Kyle Reese playing ball on what turns out to be Judgment Day (which in the reality of the series is April 21, 2011). In the present day, John and the adult Derek visit a park where the boys are playing, and John finally sees his own father, albeit as a boy younger than himself. Agent Ellison leads a raid on the motel where the Terminator Cromartie, disguised as an FBI agent, is holed up. In a chilling sequence scored to Johnny Cash's apocalyptic "When the Man Comes Around," Cromartie wipes out the entire FBI task force, leaving only Ellison alive.

"Complications"—Josh Friedman always insisted he wouldn't allow *Chronicles* to become a Terminator-of-the-week show, but it did sometimes feel like the time portal of the future had become Grand Central Station, with so many Terminators and resistance fighters traveling to the past that the concept inevitably became diluted. This second-season episode deals with that narrative problem head-on as Jesse, Derek's lover and fellow resistance fighter of the future, captures Charles Fischer, a man she insists is a traitor working for Skynet. Derek has no memory of the man, despite the fact that Jesse insists Fischer tortured Derek in their own time. Have Derek's actions in the past already changed the future, with the result that he and Jesse are actually from two different timelines? In another time loop reminiscent of the first *Terminator* movie, the older Fischer's actions in the past end up condemning his younger self to the fate we've just seen play out.

"Self Made Man"—This relatively self-contained episode reveals how the protector Terminator Cameron spends her time while everyone else is sleeping: doing research at the library. During her studies, she comes across a photo of a man she recognizes as a T-888 Terminator. Piecing together his story, she figures out that he was sent from the future in order to kill the governor of California in 2010 (a grisly little in-joke, considering who held the office at that time). A malfunction in the time-displacement equipment instead sent the T-888 to the 1920s, where he established a life as businessman Myron Stark, ruthlessly dispatching his enemies in order to secure ownership of a building where the governor would one day speak. Cameron finds him hidden inside a wall in that building, where he has been on standby for decades, and battles him to the death.

"Born to Run"—Although this wasn't intended to serve as the series finale, Friedman and company certainly knew it might end up that way by the time it was produced. It is revealed that The Turk (and by extension, its humanoid manifestation John Henry) is not the precursor to Skynet, but rather a rival, and that the T-1001 played by Shirley Manson is working against Skynet for reasons that aren't disclosed. But it is the game-changing development at episode's end that makes it memorable—and regrettable that the series would never continue. John Connor jumps ahead in time to an altered future where no members of the resistance (including Kyle and Derek Reese, as well as Cameron's human model Allison from Palmdale) know who he is. How this cliffhanger would have been resolved is anybody's guess; for a while, there was talk that the story might be resolved in a direct-to-DVD movie, but it appears that ship has sailed.

UNTANGLING THE TERMINATOR TIMELINE

A person could go crazy thinking about this," Sarah Connor concluded after pondering the paradoxes of time travel in *The Terminator*, and the process of writing this book has proved her words correct. With each new addition to the franchise, the confusion has increased exponentially. The Internet is overflowing with fan-made charts designed to sort out the *Terminator* chronology, every one of them a surefire argument starter. (One site counted no fewer than ten alternate timelines, sprouting like kudzu throughout the *Terminator* saga.) There's no real consensus to be found, but this book wouldn't be complete without its own attempt at tracking the *Terminator* timeline.

The first two films actually form a fairly straightforward time loop reminiscent of the *Planet of the Apes* series, albeit with similar unsolvable paradoxes. John Connor would never have been born had Kyle Reese not been sent back in time to save Sarah Connor and become John's father, but Kyle Reese would never have been sent back in time to save Sarah Connor if John Connor had never been born. Likewise, Cyberdyne never would have been able to develop Skynet without a computer chip from the Terminator that was sent back in time, but the Terminator never would have been sent back in time if Skynet didn't exist. (If you're already lost, feel free to stop reading this sidebar immediately.) At the end of *T2*, it appears that the Connors have prevented Skynet from ever existing . . . but if that's true, haven't they also prevented John from ever existing, in that his father will never be sent back in time?

Taking all of this into consideration, it doesn't seem like such a betrayal of James Cameron's vision when the T-850 states that Judgment Day is inevitable in *Terminator 3*. After all, it *must* be inevitable, because we know John Connor exists, and he *wouldn't* exist if Judgment Day had been averted. That is, unless you subscribe to the idea that each change made to the past results in the creation of an alternate timeline. According to this theory, there may be one universe where John Connor exists, another where he was never born, and yet another where his father was someone other than Kyle Reese. That's all well and good from an intellectual perspective, but dramatically, it feels like a cop-out. The stakes are very low indeed if there's always a timeline where everything worked out just fine.

Given those caveats, here is a timeline encompassing all four movies (but not the TV series, which is acknowledged to take place in a separate timeline and, within that, incorporates a number of alternate timelines).

1984: Sarah Connor is rescued from a time-traveling Terminator by resistance fighter Kyle Reese. During her brief time with Reese, her son John Connor is conceived. Kyle Reese dies and the Terminator is destroyed.

1985: John Connor is born.

1995: Ten-year-old John Connor is reunited with his mother after he and a protector Terminator break her out of the Pescadero Mental Hospital. A T-1000 Terminator sent from the future to kill John is destroyed. Cyberdyne Systems, the would-be birthplace of Skynet, is destroyed.

1997: The original Judgment Day is averted by the destruction of Cyberdyne. Sarah Connor dies of leukemia, per *Terminator 3*.

2004: A T-X Terminator arrives on a mission to kill the future lieutenants of resistance leader John Connor. The now-adult John, along with future wife Kate Brewster, are rescued by a reprogrammed T-850. Judgment

Day, which has not been averted but only postponed, occurs while John and Kate are safely locked away in a bomb shelter.

2018: John Connor is a rising leader of the resistance in the War Against the Machines. His wife, Kate, is pregnant. Kyle Reese is captured by Skynet but rescued by John and cyborg Marcus Wright. The first T-800 Terminators are manufactured.

2029: The resistance smashes Skynet's defense grids. Skynet sends a T-800 to 1984 and a T-1000 to 1995 in an effort to destroy John Connor. The resistance sends Kyle Reese to 1984 and a reprogrammed T-800 to 1995 to protect Connor.

2032: A T-850 assassinates John Connor, then is reprogrammed by Kate Brewster and sent back to the 2004 Judgment Day.

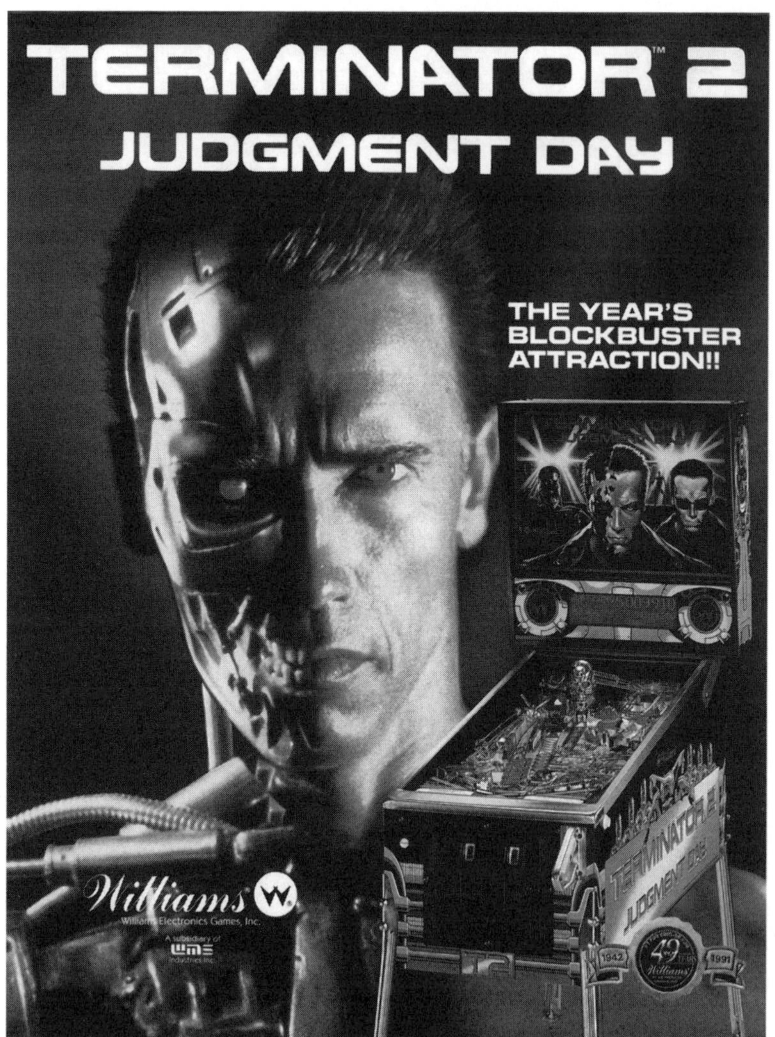

Special when lit. (Author's collection)

9

PRODUCTION LINE: *THE TERMINATOR* IN OTHER MEDIA

COMIC BOOKS

The first-ever continuation of the *Terminator* story was not James Cameron's 1991 sequel, but a 1988 product of NOW Comics, a now-defunct publisher that specialized in licensing popular movies and television shows, and churning out comic books based on them. NOW titles included *The Real Ghostbusters*, *Speed Racer*, *Married . . . with Children* (a natural for the comic-book format, we'd all have to agree), and, beginning in September 1988, a monthly series based on *The Terminator*.

The first issue of *The Terminator* comic book, written by Fred Schiller and illustrated by Tony Akins and Jim Brozman, established the setting for the series: 2031, two years after John Connor sent Kyle Reese back in time to rescue his mother. The story centers on a resistance unit known as Sarah's Slammers, which has been investigating a "flesh farm" operated by the Terminators. It seems the Machines have been breeding their own docile brand of humans in hopes of replacing the pesky rebellious kind. Sarah's Slammers find unexpected allies in a group of humans who happened to be on the Moon when Skynet launched its attack. The story continued to unfold over seventeen issues, before the series was terminated in February 1990.

By the time these comics appeared, little of the Terminator mythology we know today had been established, so there's not much in the way of continuity between the NOW series and the films or television show. That's certainly understandable, but what isn't as easily excused is the sheer shoddiness of execution on every level, from the chicken-scratch artwork to the indifferent characterizations to the unreadable (and apparently unproofreadable) dialogue. The NOW comics appear to be aimed at a younger demographic than the movie attracted, but that's no excuse for the carelessness on display here. It's as if NOW considered acquiring the rights to an existing property enough of a selling point, and that no further effort was deemed necessary.

Like the *Terminator* film rights, the comic-book license to the franchise would change hands several times after NOW released its final *Terminator* issue. Only a few months later, in September 1990, Dark Horse launched a new *Terminator* series hewing more closely to the original film's storyline. In the initial story arc "Tempest," writer John Arcudi and artists Chris Warner and Paul Guinan send a quintet of resistance fighters back in time to pursue a squadron of Terminators. In a twist that would later be revisited in *Terminator Salvation*, one of the resistance fighters is revealed to be half human, half Terminator. Although the artwork represents a substantial improvement over the NOW series, the story is a rather lackluster rehash of familiar Terminator tropes.

Under a separate license stemming from *Terminator 2*, Malibu Comics produced a pair of miniseries in the mid-'90s, with Sarah and John Connor facing off against three more Terminators. The *T2* rights were eventually acquired by Dynamite Entertainment, another comic company primarily devoted to licensing established properties. But the vast majority of Terminator comics were published by Dark Horse, which enlisted some of the biggest names in the comic-book field to further expand the Terminator universe. Frank Miller, creator of *The Dark Knight Returns*, penned a four-issue crossover series in which it is revealed that Skynet became self-aware through an encounter with the half-human, half-machine RoboCop. Matt Wagner (*Grendel*) illustrated an intriguing one-shot about a fourth Sarah Connor discovered living in Los Angeles at the time of the original *Terminator*. But perhaps the best of the lot is the six-issue miniseries *2029 to 1984*, written by Zack Whedon, brother of *Buffy the Vampire Slayer* creator Joss Whedon, and illustrated by Andy McDonald. Whedon is basically doodling in the margins of the first *Terminator* movie, but he brings welcome doses of humor, a swift, page-turning pace, and several unexpected twists to the material.

TIE-IN NOVELS

For decades before the introduction of home video, novelizations (and, briefly, photo-novels) were the only way fans could relive the stories of their favorite films or television shows on their own schedules. In 1970, author James Blish, who had adapted the entire run of the original *Star Trek* series for Bantam Books, penned the first original *Trek* tie-in novel, *Spock Must Die!* It wasn't a particularly memorable read, but it was certainly influential; in the decades that followed, the science-fiction sections of bookstores everywhere were overrun with *Star Trek* and *Star Wars* tie-in novels, expanding on the minutiae of those fictional universes and draining the wallets of their fans. These days, every popular science-fiction franchise breeds its own series of tie-in novels, and *Terminator* is no exception.

Given the tangled rights history of the Terminator franchise, it's not terribly surprising to find that two competing novel trilogies purporting to pick up the story immediately following the events of *Terminator 2: Judgment Day* appeared more or less simultaneously early in the twenty-first century. If timeline confusion is your favorite aspect of the Terminator saga, look no further than *Terminator 2: The New John Connor Chronicles* by Russell Blackford. These three action-heavy novels—*Dark Futures*, *An Evil Hour*, and *Times of Trouble*—jump around among several realities, an irritating narrative strategy that inevitably dilutes the drama. The story gets a far more worthy continuation in S. M. Stirling's *T2* trilogy, consisting of *Infiltrator*, *Rising Storm*, and *The Future War*. Stirling's books are meatier than the usual cash-in fare, and *Infiltrator* in particular does an admirable job of expanding on the characters we know and introducing several intriguing new ones, including Serena, a new kind of fully organic Terminator, and Dieter von Rossbach, a former CIA agent (and love interest for Sarah Connor) who happens to be the human model for the familiar T-800.

Following the release of *Terminator 3: Rise of the Machines*, Aaron Allston wrote the first of a pair of *T3* novels set in the post-apocalyptic future. In *Terminator Dreams*, Allston devises a clever conceit for toggling back and forth through time, as the character of resistance fighter Danny Avila discovers he can connect psychically with his younger self through dreams. John Connor and his allies attempt to harness this power in order to defeat Skynet in the past, but since we know that's not going to happen, the suspense flags in the end.

Indeed, that's a problem that plagues most third-party attempts at extending the *Terminator* franchise. The world established by the movies simply isn't as expansive as the *Star Trek* or *Star Wars* universes; there's an established timeframe in place, and a limited number of characters and situations that come into play. Anyone hoping to see the spinoff comics and novels maintain some semblance of continuity with the canonical works is only going to be driven batty by a continuous stream of Terminators pouring through the space-time continuum, and further failed attempts at derailing Skynet.

Perhaps the best approach is to focus on secondary characters, as Timothy Zahn (a veteran author of numerous *Star Wars* tie-ins) does in his *Terminator Salvation* prequel, *From the Ashes*. John Connor takes on a supporting role here, as much of the story revolves around "Moldering Lost Ashes," a settlement of survivors unconnected to the resistance. Even further afield is *Terminator Salvation: Cold War* by Greg Cox, which finds a band of survivors battling Terminators in the Alaskan wilderness.

VIDEOGAMES

More so than the comic book or the novel, the most appropriate ancillary medium for the Terminator franchise is the videogame. It's only fitting that the War Against the Machines should be played out through the use of actual machines, and the sci-fi and action trappings of the Terminator series are an ideal fit for the videogame format. Terminator games date back as far as 1990, when Bethesda Softworks released a first-person shooter for DOS. Primitive by today's standards, the game (which allowed users to play as either Kyle Reese or the Terminator) was notable at the time of its release for the size and scope of its playing field. *Terminator 2* spawned a number of videogame spinoffs, as well as an addictive pinball machine that can still be found in your finer retro gaming parlors.

Of course, most of these games were produced for now-obsolete systems, such as Game Boy and Sega Genesis. For gamers who haven't kept a museum of old consoles and handheld units on hand, several titles compatible with current systems are available. Prior to the release of the third Terminator movie, Infogrames released 2002's *The Terminator: Dawn of Fate* for the Xbox and Playstation platforms. Functioning as a prequel of sorts to the original film, *Dawn of Fate* opens in the future machine-dominated world, with the player leading Kyle Reese through a training course in preparation for his trip through time. The player controls several other characters throughout a number of missions leading to the events of the first movie, but the game is marred by confusing visuals, often changing the angle of view in midcombat.

In 2003, Atari released an adaptation of *Terminator 3: Rise of the Machines* for Xbox and Playstation, featuring voice work from the original cast. Playing as the Terminator, the goal is to complete a series of missions in the future and use the time-displacement equipment to travel to the past, after which point the game more or less mimics the plot of the movie. A poorly designed rush job, the game suffers in comparison to Atari's aptly named sequel, 2004's *Terminator 3: Redemption*. Once again, the player takes on the role of the film's T-850, but this time the gameplay is more varied (including many driving missions) and the story takes several unexpectedly time-bending twists and turns.

The most recent game, Equity Games' 2009 tie-in version of *Terminator Salvation*, is easily the most visually impressive. A third-person shooter set several years before the events of the movie, the game puts the player in John Connor's shoes (without the aid of Christian Bale, who declined to provide his voice) as he battles Skynet in post-apocalyptic Los Angeles. The environment would have made for a fun free-roaming sandbox game in the *Grand Theft*

Auto vein, but the action is strictly linear and the gameplay quickly becomes repetitive. It's a depressing reminder that most of these games, as well as the comics and tie-in novels, are viewed merely as assembly-line products by those who manufacture them.

THE FIVE MOST BLATANT *TERMINATOR* RIPOFFS

***Robot Holocaust* (1986)**—Written and directed by Tim Kincaid (*Bad Girls Dormitory*), this post-apocalyptic thriller shot in the wilds of Central Park envisions a future in which mankind has been defeated by clumsy robots, and reduced to wrestling in loincloths for the entertainment of their mechanical overlords. It's so bad, even robots made fun of it, as *Robot Holocaust* became fodder for one of the first-season episodes of *Mystery Science Theater 3000*.

***Lady Terminator* (1989)**—Foreign markets aren't always diligent about protecting the intellectual property of North American filmmakers like James Cameron. In 1990, Italian exploitation director Bruno Mattei released a movie called *Terminator 2*, which had nothing to do with Cameron's creation whatsoever. (Strangely, it was a note-for-note ripoff of *Aliens*.) And then there's this Indonesian oddity, in which the South Sea Queen takes the form of a snake and enters the vagina of an American anthropologist (the oft-nude Barbara Ann Constable), turning her into an unstoppable killing machine. *Lady Terminator* is grotesque, bizarre, and thoroughly nonsensical, yet some still prefer it to *Terminator Salvation*.

***Class of 1999* (1990)**—In 1982, director Mark L. Lester achieved moderate cult success with his punk-flavored update of the *Blackboard Jungle*, *Class of 1984*. Eight years later, for reasons that must have made sense at the time, he directed this sequel in which three "tactical education units" are dispatched to bring some law and order to the free-fire zone that is Kennedy High School. Mildly amusing for those of us who suspected all along that some of our teachers were killer robots, *Class of 1999* is sabotaged by lead teen Bradley Gregg, who suggests Coreys Haim and Feldman distilled into one unlikeable troll-boy. Nothing else in the movie is nearly as disturbing as the sight of Stacy Keach with a spiky, snow-white hockey hairdo.

***Nemesis* (1992)**—Schlock merchant Albert Pyun (*Brain Smasher . . . A Love Story*) directed this disjointed, barely coherent action cheapie about an "86.5% human" cyborg cop (Olivier Gruner) who rebels against his LAPD superiors to join the Resistance against the Machines. It's hard to say how much of the plot is derivative, since the story never makes the slightest bit of sense, but a number of signature moments are lifted directly from *The Terminator*, including a legless android pulling itself across a floor, an eyeball being removed from a cyborg's head, and, most shamelessly of all, the line "I'll be back."

***The Terminators* (2009)**—The Asylum is a small production company and distributor best known for its "mockbusters"—that is, direct-to-DVD releases shot on the cheap and packaged to resemble current blockbusters. Thus *The Da Vinci Treasure* was released around the same time as *The Da Vinci Code*, *Transmorphers* happened to find its way into video stores just as *Transformers* was opening in theaters, and *The Terminators* made its debut a month before the arrival of *Terminator Salvation*. The story, such as it is, concerns a rebellion of robot workers known as TRs on the *2001*-esque Ellison Space Station (wink-wink). The TRs make their escape to Earth, where the fate of civilization is in the hands of the dopiest people on the planet. Fans of violent neck snapping and billowing plumes of blood will find what they're looking for here, but is it really worth enduring the porn-level acting and thrift-store visual effects?

THE MUSIC OF THE TERMINATOR

What does composer Brad Fiedel have in common with James Cameron, besides the fact that *The Terminator* served as a breakthrough for both of them? Before making it big, each toiled away on a low-budget *Jaws* ripoff. Cameron, of course, directed that great flying-fish movie *Piranha II*, while Fiedel supplied the music for the pornographic parody *Gums*, starring Brother Theodore as Captain Carl Clitoris. Fiedel, a former keyboardist for Hall & Oates, primarily composed for TV movies before Cameron tapped him to provide the score for *The Terminator.*

Fiedel's remarkably varied electronic score ranged from the throbbing synth suspense of "Tunnel Chase" to the self-explanatory "Love Scene," but it's most memorable for its main theme, with its insistent, metallic clanging—"a mechanical man and his heartbeat," as the composer describes it in the *Other Voices* documentary included on the *Terminator* DVD. That heartbeat would become the signature sound of the franchise, instantly conjuring the image of the Terminator whenever it's heard. The rest of the *Terminator* soundtrack was not quite as indelible. Three forgettable pop-rock tunes credited to the one-time-only band "Tahnee Cain and Tryanglz" sound like Pat Benatar outtakes, and the cheesy synth-pop track "Intimacy" is easily the most dated element of the movie.

Fiedel returned for *Terminator 2* with an even more expansive synthesizer score, but that soundtrack is probably best known for the inclusion of "You Could Be Mine," a new track from Guns N' Roses, the biggest rock band in the world at the time. Arnold Schwarzenegger appeared as the Terminator in the music video for the song, in which he has orders to kill the band but, in the end, spares Axl Rose (a decision the rest of the band members, all long since replaced by Rose, may now regret). *T2* is also famous for its use of George Thorogood's "Bad to the Bone" in the scene in which the Terminator acquires his biker gear. Even in 1991, that was one of the most overused soundtrack songs of all, a point James Cameron acknowledges on the *T2* DVD commentary, while noting that he just couldn't resist.

Like Cameron, Fiedel did not return for the subsequent Terminator outings. *Terminator 3* was scored by Marco Beltrami (*The Hurt Locker*), *Terminator Salvation* by Danny Elfman (*Batman*), and the television series by Bear McCreary (*Battlestar Galactica*). But no matter who the composer, you can be sure Fiedel's "mechanical man and his heartbeat" will surface at some point on the soundtrack. No *Terminator* is complete without it.

"I've seen things you people wouldn't believe." (Warner Bros./Photofest)

10

TECH NOIR: THE INFLUENCE OF *THE TERMINATOR*

BLADE RUNNER AND THE BIRTH OF A SUBGENRE

When in *The Terminator* James Cameron called the night-club where Sarah Connor hides from her pursuer Tech Noir, it wasn't simply because he thought that would be a cool name for a bar. In typically self-aggrandizing Cameron fashion, he was both announcing the birth of new film genre and anointing his own film as that genre's signature work. In simplest terms, "tech noir" is a blend of the science-fiction and film-noir genres—a blend that certainly existed long before cameras rolled on *The Terminator.* Jean-Luc Godard specifically set out to combine sci-fi with noir in 1965's *Alphaville*, and cases could be made for even earlier films, such as Don Siegel's shadowy 1956 take on *Invasion of the Body Snatchers*, or even Fritz Lang's silent-era epic *Metropolis*. But if one movie could be credited with kicking off the tech-noir boom that continues to this day, it would have to be Ridley Scott's 1982 magnum opus *Blade Runner*.

Based on Philip K. Dick's novel *Do Androids Dream of Electric Sheep?*, the screenplay for *Blade Runner* had been kicking around under various titles for years before it came to Scott's attention. As far back as 1969, then-unknown director Martin Scorsese had expressed interest in adapting the novel for the screen, though he never got as far as optioning the book. After a 1974 option by Herb Jaffe Associations lapsed, screenwriter Hampton Fancher and actor Brian Kelly acquired the rights from Dick, and Fancher began work on a screenplay adaptation. Dick's novel had been described by several interested parties as "unfilmable," and as Fancher's efforts to complete the script known variously as *Android*, *Mechanismo*, and *Dangerous Days* dragged on, it began to look like this might be true.

Although at first reluctant to follow up *Alien* with another science-fiction film, director Ridley Scott joined the project in 1980. Scott brought in David Peoples to rewrite Fancher's script, then began the process of visualizing a futuristic world unlike any other. Set in the Los Angeles of 2019, the movie now known as *Blade Runner* depicts an overpopulated society where human-like androids known as "replicants" are used as slave labor in off-world colonies but banned on Earth. The script by Fancher and Peoples incorporates these science-fiction elements into an archetypal noir storyline. A world-weary detective named Deckard (Harrison Ford) takes on one last case: the "retirement" of four of these replicants, led by the dangerous Roy Batty (Rutger Hauer). In the course of his investigation, he meets and falls in love with Rachael (Sean Young), a replicant with implanted memories who had always believed herself to be human. Charged with retiring Rachael as well, Deckard must choose between his heart and his duty.

The story of *Blade Runner* is not nearly as compelling, however, as the world which it inhabits. Having assembled a formidable team of artists, special-effects gurus, and futurists, including Syd Mead and Douglas Trumbull, Scott began designing a densely layered, meticulously detailed future Los Angeles that would set the standard for tech-noir cityscapes. *Blade Runner*'s L.A. is a congested, multicultural metropolis festooned with neon and large-scale advertising (mostly for companies that have gone belly-up since the film's release, demonstrating the limits of Scott's prescience), a city of perpetual night, shrouded in fog and rain. It bears much more resemblance to the vertical cities of the Far East than the ever-sprawling Los Angeles of today, but it's an undeniably moody and entrancing tech-noir setting. Scott enhances the noir vibe with plumes of cigarette smoke and shadows from overhead ceiling fans—and in the original theatrical cut, at least, with Harrison Ford's voice-over narration. This last addition was a step too far in the direction of pastiche, if not outright parody; rather than world-weary or hard-boiled, Ford sounds sarcastic and bored. The subtext of every line seems to be "I can't believe you're making me read this crap," and eventually Scott agreed, cutting the narration for his director's cut (as well as for subsequent cuts, all of which are gathered in a four-disc DVD boxed set).

Looking at *Blade Runner* today, it's easy to believe that Ridley Scott lavished every ounce of his creativity and filmmaking savvy on the endeavor. (His generally underwhelming filmography since 1982 certainly suggests he had precious little left in the tank after completing *Blade Runner*.) It's not just the striking look of the film, but the overall entrancing mood of the piece. It unfolds slowly, and may prove frustrating to first-time viewers, but give yourself over to its beguiling rhythms and it can lull you into a dreamlike state of total immersion in the film's unique world. When that happens, it hardly matters that there's no particularly complex plotting or compelling mystery to be unraveled. (Even the much-debated notion of whether Deckard himself is a replicant carries little emotional weight in the end.)

Although James Cameron did not create his own future Los Angeles in *The Terminator*, he certainly put the existing city streets and alleyways to effective noir-ish use. (It almost never rains in Southern California, but in film noir, the night streets of L.A. are always slick and shimmery nonetheless.) Cameron has never denied the influence of Scott's film on his own, and together, *Blade Runner* and *The Terminator* set the stage for a new wave of science-fiction films less concerned with space battles and alien creatures than with dark explorations of identity and reality, set against moody backdrops suffused with paranoia and technophobia.

Perhaps the purest distillation of the tech-noir aesthetic outside of *Blade Runner* is *Dark City*, a 1998 feature directed by Alex Proyas (*The Crow*). A box-office failure upon its release, and generally ignored by critics (with the notable exception of Roger Ebert, who was so taken with the film that he recorded a commentary track for the DVD release), *Dark City*'s reputation has improved over the years as it has accumulated a devoted cult following. The aptly titled film takes place in another city of perpetual night, but this isn't Los Angeles or any other recognizable metropolis from the real world. It's a mix-and-match dreamscape drawn from the memories of its inhabitants, made up of design elements from different eras throughout the twentieth century, drawing inspiration from Fritz Lang's *Metropolis*, as well as *Blade Runner*, the Gotham City of Tim Burton's *Batman*, the paintings of Edward Hopper, and any number of films from the '30s and '40s in the film-noir and German Expressionist styles.

Against this intoxicating backdrop, a story that begins as classic film noir and winds up as the wildest of science fiction unfolds. A man (Rufus Sewell) wakes up in a bathtub in an old hotel, with no memory of his past, and finds the corpse of a murdered prostitute in the room. A creepy doctor (Kiefer Sutherland channeling Peter Lorre) calls, warning him that men are on their way to get him. "Men" is actually a misnomer; as we later learn, these are the Strangers, extraterrestrial beings who have taken over the bodies of dead humans in order to study our kind. The Strangers possess a power they call "tuning," which allows them to transform the shape of the city, transfer memories between bodies, and even stop time. The amnesiac man, who learns his name is John Murdoch, discovers that he has these same powers, which he uses to escape the Strangers, evade a detective (William Hurt) investigating him for multiple murders, and find his estranged wife (Jennifer Connelly). All the while he is haunted by a vague childhood memory of a place called Shell Beach, a blue-sky oasis out of reach from this sunless urban nightmare.

Dark City is at its best (and most noir-ish) in its first half, when it's setting up its mysteries and allowing us to soak in the richly atmospheric world Proyas has created. The more we learn about the Strangers, who look like the demons from *Hellraiser* by way of F. W. Murnau, the loopier the movie gets. Still, *Dark City* is a crucial step in the development of tech noir and a film that repays repeated viewings.

Exploring much the same territory, albeit to considerably less fascinating effect, is 1999's *The Thirteenth Floor*. Based loosely on the

1964 novel *Simulacron-3* by Daniel F. Galouye (which had already been adapted for German television by Rainer Werner Fassbinder), the film directed by Josef Rusnak features a virtual world meticulously recreating 1937 Los Angeles. The creator of this virtual reality has been murdered, and one of his programmers (Craig Bierko) is a suspect in the crime. Bierko is able to enter the virtual world by jacking into an avatar of himself, through which he can interact with the sim-people of a lushly rendered '30s L.A. Rusnak's attempts at lending a noir atmosphere to the proceedings are only moderately successful, but the late revelation of virtual worlds within worlds might have resonated more strongly had the movie not opened while *The Matrix* (which we'll discuss shortly) was still in theaters.

Some exercises in tech noir are less interested in recasting the signature visual style of film noir in a science-fiction context than in giving some of the genre's narrative tropes a technological upgrade. In the case of Andrew Niccol's 1997 directorial debut *Gattaca* (which Niccol also wrote), the central plot device is that time-honored staple at the heart of such noir classics as *Detour* and *Dark Passage*, in which the protagonist assumes another man's identity. In the near-future world of *Gattaca*, however, this is not a simple matter of swiping a dead man's wallet or even having reconstructive facial surgery. Vincent Freeman (Ethan Hawke) has been marked since birth by his own genetic code.

Although he's dreamed since childhood of traveling to space, Vincent has no chance of doing so, as he is an "in-valid"—meaning that a scan of his DNA at birth revealed a high probability that a heart defect would limit his lifespan to little more than thirty years. In order to realize his dream, Vincent assumes the identity of Jerome Morrow (Jude Law), a man born with all the right genetics, but none of Vincent's drive. Confined to a wheelchair following a car accident, Jerome sells blood, urine, skin, and hair samples to Vincent, so that he may pass himself off as a "valid" at the Gattaca Aerospace Corporation. *Gattaca* delves further into noir territory when one of Gattaca's executives is murdered on the premises, prompting an investigation by the authorities, one of whom is Vincent's real brother.

Niccol's visual scheme isn't as noir-influenced as some of the films discussed in this chapter. He does evoke the 1940s in fashion and decor to some degree, but the set design recalls the concrete futurism of the '70s more than the urban infernos of noir, and his images tend to be infused with shades of yellow and green rather than the dark, neon-flecked palette of other tech noirs. Though *Gattaca* offers plenty of food for thought on the subject of eugenics, and explores the same sort of fate-versus-free-will themes as the *Terminator* films, the film is marred by some overly expository voice-over narration and a routine murder mystery.

ROBOCOP: THE POST-TERMINATOR CYBORG

One of the many offshoots of film noir was the brand of gritty urban cop drama that flourished in the '70s and early '80s. Director Paul Verhoeven gave that genre a subversive twist with his 1987 hit *RoboCop*, a satirical sci-fi actioner that recasts the cyborg as a corporate-sponsored law-enforcement tool. In Verhoeven's vision, the sleek city of the future is promised but yet to be built; meanwhile, Old Detroit continues to crumble into crime-ridden chaos. The police department has been privatized and is now under control of the giant corporation Omni Consumer Products. After an effort to build a completely robotic police force suffers a setback, an alternative plan is put into motion: rebuilding a human cop as a cyborg.

The opportunity arises when Officer Murphy (Peter Weller) is critically injured and left for dead after a shootout with Detroit crime boss Clarence Boddicker (Kurtwood Smith) and his gang. Under the direction of OCP exec Bob Morton (Miguel Ferrer), Murphy is reborn as RoboCop, a heavily armored—and heavily armed—cybernetic organism programmed to serve and protect. (RoboCop's initial activation plays out through the same sort of digitally enhanced first-person point of view James Cameron often employed for the Terminator.) With the help of partner Anne Lewis (Nancy Allen), RoboCop gradually rediscovers his humanity, even as he battles a corrupt alliance between Boddicker and OCP president Dick Jones (Ronny Cox).

What gives *RoboCop* its caustic kick is Verhoeven's depiction of the corporate-controlled future, which feels more relevant now than ever. Verhoeven peppers the film with snippets of satirical newscasts in which smiling anchors cheerfully deliver reports of horrific violence and with advertisements for bigger, louder products (like the Porsche 6000 SUX) that hardly seem far-fetched at all. The sharp contrast between the gleaming OCP headquarters towering over the city and the urban blight below encapsulates the worst-case-scenario endpoint of consumerist culture and unchecked corporate greed. *RoboCop* is certainly no serious thesis statement on these issues, but as cartoonishly violent action movies of the '80s go, it's more thought-provoking and self-aware than most. Like *The Terminator* before it, *RoboCop* was successful enough to spawn several sequels, a short-lived television series, and many merchandising offshoots, but the longer the RoboCop saga played out, the closer it came to becoming the sort of thing it satirized in the first place.

Released the same year as *RoboCop*, the underseen gem *The Hidden* mines a similar satirical vein, albeit with aliens in place of cyborgs. Foreshadowing his role as spacey Agent Dale Cooper on *Twin Peaks*, Kyle MacLachlan stars as an FBI agent sent to Los Angeles to track down a dangerous criminal. As we learn early in the movie, the criminal is actually an insectoid alien from another world occupying a deceased human body. The alien has no particular master plan to take over our planet or enslave humanity; it simply wants to enjoy all the pleasures of American life circa the late twentieth century, including but not limited to sex, violence, and rock 'n' roll. Once a body is all used up, the alien simply discards it and selects a new one, making it very difficult to capture or kill.

In fact, MacLachlan is the only one equipped to kill the creature because, as his peculiar, dislocated behavior suggests, he is also an alien. The dynamic between these two strangers in a strange land—the destructive villain oblivious to the harm he causes to people and property, and his earnest pursuer who must convince an ordinary American that his outlandish tale is true—is more than a little reminiscent of *The Terminator*, as is the contemporary Los Angeles battleground. (L.A. inevitably attracts freaks, it seems, whether from the future or a distant star.) *The Hidden* is no mere ripoff, however, as director Jack Sholder invests his film with B-movie brio and sardonic jabs at the hedonistic Hollywood lifestyle.

Futuristic robots figure into two films from directors already associated with tech noir—Alex Proyas (*Dark City*) and Jonathan Mostow (*Terminator 3*)—with less than impressive results. Proyas turned to the bible of robot stories, by Isaac Asimov, for 2004's *I, Robot,* but aside from appropriating the three rules of robotics from that classic collection, his film has little in common with its source material. Instead, it's a fairly standard Will Smith action picture, complete with all the glib one-liners and empty digital effects we've come to expect from such a package. Mostow's *Surrogates* is slightly more interesting in concept, if not execution, as Bruce Willis stars as an FBI agent investigating a series of murders in a vaguely futuristic society where most citizens choose to live their lives through younger, fitter robot surrogates. There's a sly commentary about our image-driven culture and propensity for reinventing ourselves through online cyber-personas here somewhere, but it's buried under standard-issue chase scenes and a run-of-the-mill mystery.

CYBERPUNK ON THE SCREEN

Even as *The Terminator* reached movie screens in 1984, a new novel by William Gibson was taking the world of literary science fiction by storm. The story of a hacker hired to pull off a virtual heist, *Neuromancer* has been roundly hailed as a seminal work of cyberpunk, a subgenre of sci-fi wherein "high tech meets low life." Several efforts at bringing *Neuromancer* to the screen failed over the years, but that didn't stop Hollywood, never wanting to miss out on a hot trend, from making movies about cyberspace, hacking, and virtual reality before really understanding what they were.

Of course, most of us in the audience didn't understand much of it, either. In 1984 we were introduced to Max Headroom, ostensibly the world's first computer-generated character. Although widely assumed to be an entirely digital creation, this Coca-Cola pitchman and British chat show host was actually character actor Matt Frewer in a rubber mask, made to appear more electronic with the help of squiggly animated backdrops and stutter-step editing. Ersatz as he was, Max did play a role in one of the earliest attempts at bringing cyberpunk to the screen: the TV-movie *Max Headroom: 20 Minutes into the Future*, which also spawned a short-lived ABC series. Frewer did double-duty as Network 23 reporter Edison Carter, who stumbles onto a conspiracy involving subliminal and potentially fatal "blip-verts" being introduced into his own network's programming, and his digital alter ego Max. The series was perhaps too far ahead of its time, as it failed to catch on with audiences beyond a minor cult following.

As laughable early attempts at cinematic cyberpunk go, 1992's *The Lawnmower Man* is in a class by itself. Ostensibly based on a Stephen King story to which it bears no resemblance (the author successfully sued to have his name removed from the credits), this film co-written and directed by Brett Leonard reimagines *Flowers for Algernon* for the digital age, as scientist Pierce Brosnan makes simpleton Jeff Fahey smarter with drugs and virtual reality. The then-revolutionary CGI segments consist mainly of colorful blobs and geometric shapes, suggesting what it might have looked like had James Cameron tried to make *Avatar* with a Lite-Brite.

Leonard returned to the cyberpunk well for 1995's *Virtuosity*, with scant improvement. Russell Crowe supplies enough ham for a six-foot sub as a virtual criminal who escapes cyberspace to wreak havoc in the real world, while Denzel Washington searches for a new agent. Faring slightly better that same year was *Johnny Mnemonic*, which at least had the advantage of being based on a William Gibson short story. Keanu Reeves stars as a courier who transports sensitive data via an implant in his brain, a contrivance seemingly less efficient than Rapidshare or Dropbox, but more conducive to action sequences involving the yakuza. Speaking of the Japanese, their anime has always been ahead of the curve when it comes to cutting-edge sci-fi concepts, and cyberpunk is no exception. Mamoru Oshii's 1995 feature *Ghost in the Shell*, based on the manga series of the same name, is a densely detailed, often lyrical, sometimes impenetrable animated thriller about cyborg cops hunting a dangerous hacker. It was also a huge influence on two filmmaking brothers from Chicago when it came time to make their own cyber-themed movie—one that would also owe a debt to *The Terminator*.

THE MATRIX AND PHILDICKIAN CINEMA

For all of *Blade Runner*'s virtues, it's not particularly successful at translating Philip K. Dick's sensibility to the screen. And for all of *Total Recall*'s box-office success, it barely even tried to capture that "phildickian" essence. (*Phildickian* is one of those great made-up words of the Internet age that means exactly what it sounds like it means—that which possesses qualities associated with the work of Philip K. Dick.) In fact, with one or two exceptions, the most phildickian movies to date were not based on any of the author's works. For reasons that may have been related to millennial angst or may have been completely coincidental, the late 1990s were a hotbed for films exploring questions of identity and reality through a science-fiction framework.

Perhaps the most prophetic of these films (so far, at least) was Peter Weir's 1998 film *The Truman Show*, starring Jim Carrey as a man who learns that his entire life has been spent in front of hidden cameras and broadcast around the world, twenty-four hours a day. Arriving as the reality-television genre was in its infancy, the film (scripted by *Gattaca* director Andrew Niccol) anticipated TV shows like *Big Brother* and reality stars like the Kardashians, who appear to live their entire lives in front of the camera. At least today's reality-television participants are aware their lives are being taped and broadcast (even if they sometimes seem to forget); Carrey's Truman Burbank has to contend with the fact that his entire life has been a simulated reality existing for the entertainment of others. It's a phildickian predicament, to be sure—and one the man himself had explored in his novel *Time Out of Joint*.

The following year saw the release of another film in which the protagonist learns he has spent his entire life inside a simulated reality—a blockbuster owing as much to *The Terminator* as *Time Out of Joint* and a dozen other influences, including anime, martial-arts movies, mythology, philosophy, comic books, and cyberpunk. That all of these elements could somehow coalesce into a crowd-pleasing entertainment that would spawn two sequels is a tribute to its creators, Andy and Larry (now Lana) Wachowski. That film was, of course, *The Matrix*.

Keanu Reeves (who, with his role here, as well as his turns in *Johnny Mnemonic* and *A Scanner Darkly*, is clearly the Bogart of tech noir) stars as Neo, a hacker and cubicle drone who learns that his entire existence has been a virtual reality constructed by computers that enslaved humanity following a familiar-sounding War of the Machines. Neo is recruited by the human resistance led by Morpheus (Laurence Fishburne), who reveals that most of humanity spends its entire lifetime wired into a gigantic power source for the machines. While their bodies are used as batteries in the late twenty-second century, their minds are plugged into the Matrix, a meticulous re-creation of life circa 1999. Like John Connor, Neo is The One—the prophesied leader of the resistance that will bring down the tyranny of the machines.

It's easy to enjoy *The Matrix* even if you can't take its dorm-room existentialism seriously, particularly if you identify with the Joe Pantoliano character (who prefers the comforts of the Matrix to the harsh reality of the machine-dominated future) and consider the Morpheus character a pompous gasbag. The Wachowskis have synthesized their disparate interests into a fluid, often innovative action-adventure incorporating a engrossing mythology drawing on pop-culture milestones ranging from *Alice in Wonderland* to *Neuromancer*. The sibling directors' sure touch would fail them in the two sequels shot back-to-back, *The Matrix Reloaded* and *Matrix Revolutions*, which led the series down a rabbit hole of ponderous exposition and diminishing returns.

Far less heralded than *The Matrix*, but more intriguing than its initial critical and popular reaction would suggest, is David Cronenberg's 1999 exercise in phildickian cinema, *eXistenZ*. Cronenberg had dabbled in cyberpunk and tech noir before, with such films as *Scanners* and *Videodrome*, but *eXistenZ* is yet another pre-millennial dip into simulated reality, this time through the medium of videogames. Jennifer Jason Leigh is an acclaimed game designer testing her latest work, eXistenZ, with a focus group. In typical

Cronenbergian fashion, the virtual world of her game is entered not through sleek, futuristic machinery, but with the aid of slimy organic pods connected via umbilical cords directly into the gamers' bodies. Throughout the bizarre game, the participants find themselves questioning the borders between fantasy and reality, right up through the film's final line: "Are we still in the game?" *EXistenZ* may not be Cronenberg's most substantial work, but it succeeds brilliantly in creating a unique, brain-teasing environment and a structure that adheres closer to videogame logic than to traditional narrative.

Perhaps the least likely director/star pairing to ever dabble in phildickian cinema, the *Jerry Maguire* duo of Cameron Crowe and Tom Cruise reteamed in 2001 for an American adaptation of the 1997 Spanish film *Abre los Ojos* (*Open Your Eyes*), directed and co-written by Alejandro Amenábar. In *Vanilla Sky*, Cruise plays a playboy heir to a publishing fortune who falls in love at first sight with guileless Penelope Cruz (reprising her role from the Spanish version), much to the displeasure of his "friend with benefits" Cameron Diaz. A distraught Diaz crashes her car with Cruise in the passenger seat, killing herself and disfiguring his face in the process. Cruise finds himself in a confusing dreamlike reality of clashing identities, which is eventually explained through a clever variation on the old "he's-been-dead-the-whole-time" trope. Most critics didn't appreciate Crowe's attempt at stretching his creative muscles, but in retrospect, *Vanilla Sky* is surprisingly engaging and affecting, with Diaz's unsettling performance a particular standout. The following year, Cruise would star in an actual Philip K. Dick adaptation: *Minority Report*, directed by Steven Spielberg. Set in a futuristic society where privacy is a distant memory, this film concerns a "pre-crime" cop (Cruise) who is able to stop murders before they happen with the help of psychic mutants called "pre-cogs." When Cruise himself is flagged as a future murderer, he attempts to clear his name and bring down the system he believed in right up until the system came for him. There's more than a little *Logan's Run* in Spielberg's take on the material, which predictably offers a far more feel-good conclusion than Dick himself provided.

If asked to name one filmmaker whose sensibility most closely aligns with that of Philip K. Dick, most phildickian scholars would likely choose Charlie Kaufman. From his first produced screenplay, the fresh, funny *Being John Malkovich*, through his directorial debut, the ambitious, emotionally draining *Synecdoche, New York*, Kaufman's work has consistently pushed the boundaries of cinema in its exploration of the nature of reality. Kaufman's most Dickian work is his screenplay for the masterful sci-fi romance *Eternal Sunshine of the Spotless Mind*, a 2004 film directed by Michel Gondry. The story of a scorned lover (Jim Carrey) who undergoes an experimental procedure to remove all memory of his ex (Kate Winslet) from his mind, *Eternal Sunshine* is wildly imaginative, with a core of melancholy and heartbreak that's hard to shake off. Kaufman's films are admittedly a bit far afield of the *Terminator* franchise, but anyone with a taste for adventurous, science-fiction-tinged filmmaking should not hesitate to seek them out.

BATTLESTAR GALACTICA: TECH NOIR ON THE SMALL SCREEN

When the original *Battlestar Galactica* series premiered on ABC in September of 1978, it was widely dismissed as a *Star Wars* ripoff, and rightly so. Created by Glen A. Larson, the show initially drew strong ratings for its Lucas-esque space battles between the daredevil heroes of Galactica (including Han Solo clone Starbuck, played by Dirk Benedict) and the gleaming metallic Cylons that sought their destruction. As the series settled into a dreary space opera and began recycling its special effects and storylines, the audience dwindled. The show was canceled after only one season, although it did return briefly in the cost-cutting form of *Galactica 1980*.

The series might have remained a half-remembered slice of '70s nostalgia had the Sci Fi Channel (now known as SyFy) not approached writer Ronald D. Moore (*Star Trek: Deep Space Nine*) and producer David Eick (*American Gothic*) about reimagining *Galactica* as a miniseries. Moore responded by transplanting elements of character and plot from the original into a darker, more refined context. His *Battlestar Galactica* began decades after a War Against the Machines, in which man's own creations, the Cylons, turned against him. As the miniseries begins, no Cylon has been seen in forty years, and the citizens of Caprica and the other eleven colonies are unaware that the metallic "toasters" they remember have been superseded by twelve Cylon models indistinguishable from humans. After a surprise nuclear attack by the Cylons wipes out most of humanity, the survivors flee in a space caravan led by the obsolete *Battlestar Galactica*, commanded by William Adama (Edward James Olmos). Their goal, as in the original series, is to find a new home on the legendary thirteenth colony, known as Earth.

Despite some misplaced whining from fans of the '70s series about the casting of a woman (Katee Sackhoff) as Starbuck, the miniseries was a ratings success, prompting the Sci Fi Channel to proceed with a full-fledged weekly series. What unfolded over the course of four seasons and seventy-five episodes was a mature, intelligent, and often gripping saga that paralleled many of the real-world concerns of its era, including terrorism, imperialism, religious fundamentalism, and technophobia. It is also virtually alone among depictions of war between human and machine in its suggestion that there may be a path to peace that doesn't involve completely wiping out one side or the other—a defiantly post-*Terminator* view of our future. *Galactica* faltered a bit in the end, with its mysteries giving way to muddled mysticism in the series finale, "Daybreak" (and the prequel series *Caprica*, dealing with the creation of the Cylons, was fatally flawed from the start), but as a whole, it may be the finest sustained piece of tech-noir entertainment to date.

FIVE PHILIP K. DICK ADAPTATIONS YOU MIGHT HAVE MISSED

***Impostor* (2001)**—Originally intended as the middle segment of an anthology film consisting of three science-fiction shorts, *Impostor* was promoted to feature-length status on the strength of its early production footage. This was probably a mistake, as this movie based on Dick's short story of the same name has just about enough plot to sustain the original forty-minute version (which is available as a bonus feature on the DVD release). Gary Sinise stars as a weapons designer accused by detective Vincent D'Onofrio of being a replicant created by enemy aliens from Alpha Centauri. The premise is ripe for an exploration of Dick's pet themes of paranoia and identity confusion, but too much of the feature version's running time is dedicated to routine chase scenes.

***Paycheck* (2003)**—Hong Kong action director John Woo might seem to be a poor match for Philip K. Dick, but he actually proves fairly adept at establishing a mood of paranoia and intrigue early in this adaptation of the short story of the same name. Ben Affleck stars as a reverse engineer hired by major corporations in order to steal (and often improve upon) the competition's latest technology. After each job, Affleck's memory is wiped as a security measure. Everything goes awry after Affleck takes the proverbial one last job and finds himself with only an envelope full of everyday objects, which he must use to evade capture after being implicated in a crime he didn't commit. Oddly enough for a Woo film, *Paycheck* falters badly in its action sequences, which feel like tired retreads of scenes he's done better in earlier films.

***A Scanner Darkly* (2006)**—In a way, watching Richard Linklater's trippy take on Dick is like discovering a long-forgotten midnight movie from the 1970s. At the same time, this animated adaptation is utterly state-of-the-art, with themes that resonate with our up-to-the-minute concerns about security, privacy, and our government. Linklater's facility with fringe characters and conspiracy-minded kooks dates all the way back to his 1991 debut *Slacker*, and *Scanner* centers on a collection of oddballs and burnouts who could be Orange County cousins to the Austinites of that film. Employing the Rotoscope animation technique he first used on *Waking Life*, Linklater effectively renders the disorientation and paranoia of the drug-addled characters, notably Keanu Reeves' undercover cop, who learns he's conducting surveillance on himself. Of all the Dick adaptations, it is *Scanner* that most effectively translates the mind-bending aspects of the author's work to the screen.

***Next* (2007)**—Those who know Dick's work only from its movie adaptations could be forgiven for getting the impression that the author was best known for his extensive and elaborate chase scenes. This Nicolas Cage vehicle directed by the once-promising Lee Tamahori (*Once Were Warriors*) is another case in point. Taking almost nothing from the novelette on which it's based (*The Golden Man*), *Next* does at least feature an intriguing hook: Cage's character can see two minutes into the future, allowing him to stay one step ahead of the FBI agent (Julianne Moore) trying to harness his power to fight terrorism. The movie's first half hour or so makes fun use of this twist, but eventually *Next* degenerates into just another action movie in which Cage indulges all his hammiest impulses.

***The Adjustment Bureau* (2011)**—George Nolfi's directorial debut has almost nothing to do with Dick's 1954 short story "Adjustment Team," aside from the central notion that our reality is constantly being manipulated by forces beyond our understanding. Matt Damon stars as an up-and-coming politician whose career is derailed by a scandal. While preparing to give his concession speech, he falls in love at first sight with Emily Blunt (giving a very fall-in-lovable performance), a development that does not sit well with the fedora-wearing caseworkers of the Adjustment Bureau. Their chairman has decreed that Damon and Blunt must be kept apart, as part of The Plan, but despite their manipulations, true love keeps prevailing. The "love conquers all" theme is hard to reconcile with Dick's bleak worldview, but that doesn't prevent *The Adjustment Bureau* from being one of the more lively, entertaining adaptations of his work.

THE ALL-DAY ROLAND EMMERICH DISASTER-THON

Push the James Cameron aesthetic to its worst-case-scenario limits and you might well end up with the films of Roland Emmerich. The German-born director has developed a reputation as the master of "disaster porn" with a string of blockbusters heavily reliant on CGI effects, oversized images of destruction, and a cavalier approach to the finer points of characterization and coherent storytelling. In order to give you, the reader, an immersive yet safe and expeditious Emmerich experience, the author subjected himself and his unwitting canine companion to a fourteen-hour marathon of the filmmaker's work.

9:00 a.m.: *Universal Soldier*—This *Terminator*-derivative 1992 action flick pits Jean-Claude Van Damme and Dolph Lundgren against each other as genetically modified super-soldiers reanimated from the corpses of two dead Vietnam grunts. As signified by his necklace of severed ears, Lundgren is the bad guy.

DESTRUCTION TALLY: A gas station, a prison bus, an eighteen-wheeler, most of a motel, and a small Vietnamese village.

10:50 a.m. *Independence Day*—An alien invasion is averted with a computer virus—a clever twist on *War of the Worlds*, as long as you ignore the unlikelihood of visitors from another planet using an Apple operating system. (Steve Jobs' influence was immense, but that's pushing it.) An all-star cast is on hand to enact some of the most egregious stereotypes ever assembled.

DESTRUCTION TALLY: The Empire State Building, the White House, the Capitol . . . basically all of downtown Los Angeles, New York, and Washington, D.C., along with an air force base, various choppers, bombers, fighter jets, and an alien mothership and all of its babyships. The dog survives.

1:20 p.m. *Godzilla*—Updating the Japanese monster movies of the '50s using *Jurassic Park* technology in lieu of actors in rubber suits must have seemed like a good idea at the time. With CGI still in its relative infancy in the late '90s, however, the digital Godzilla wasn't always an improvement on its low-tech predecessors, and Emmerich was forced to use darkness and heavy rain to disguise its deficiencies. The giant lizard's repetitive Manhattan rampage raises only one compelling question: How did Godzilla get to New York, anyway? Did he take the Panama Canal?

DESTRUCTION TALLY: The Chrysler Building, the Flatiron Building, the MetLife Building, Madison Square Garden, the Brooklyn Bridge, a Japanese freighter, three fishing boats, a submarine, and Matthew Broderick's movie career.

3:50 p.m.: *The Day After Tomorrow*—In Emmerich's hands, catastrophic climate change is just another giant lizard or alien invasion—an excuse to render cinematic destruction on a massive scale. Here Emmerich confuses global-warming opponents with a worldwide weather event that results in tornadoes, massive tidal waves, and plummeting temperatures. Dennis Quaid is a climatologist who must rescue his son Jake Gyllenhaal, who is trapped in the New York Public Library, now surrounded by a frozen wasteland.

DESTRUCTION TALLY: The Hollywood sign (destroyed by a tornado in what might have been a subversive sight gag in the hands of a more subtle filmmaker), downtown Los Angeles (again), New York City (flooded, then frozen), and eventually the entire Northern Hemisphere. The dog survives.

6:05 p.m.: *10,000 B.C.* —Emmerich's 2011 feature *Anonymous*, which purported to tell the truth behind the authorship of Shakespeare's works, was widely criticized for taking liberties with history. It was certainly not the first time Emmerich ran afoul of sticklers for accuracy, as this prehistoric epic offers a unique explanation for the secret of the pyramids: they were built using exploited woolly-mammoth labor. It's hard to get too bogged down in the pesky details of whether early man battled saber-toothed tigers, however, as no matter what is ostensibly happening onscreen in this CGI-drenched folly, it all looks like actors running in place in front of a green screen.

DESTRUCTION TALLY: There's not much destruction, given that there wasn't much constructed at the time the movie is set. A couple of pyramids suffer minor damage.

8:20 p.m.: ***2012***—Emmerich's apocalyptic vision finds its fullest expression in yet another tale of the end times (this time brought about by solar flares causing the Earth's core to overheat). All sense and sensibility are abandoned in favor of pure sensationalism and spectacle as limo driver/failed novelist John Cusack frantically struggles to deliver his estranged family to the super-sized arks built to keep the 1 percent alive after the fall. As narrative, Emmerich's films fail on nearly every level—this one in particular would have you believe that the destruction of almost all life on the planet is inconsequential as long as this one terrible family survives—but his flair for gigantism is undeniable. Individual images—spaceships the size of cities, tidal waves rolling down Fifth Avenue, Godzilla tangled in the suspension of the Brooklyn Bridge—have the power of nightmares. It's a shame those images are surrounded by such dreadful movies.

DESTRUCTION TALLY: Yellowstone Park, Los Angeles (for the third time in the Emmerich oeuvre), the White House (for the second time), Rio's Christ the Redeemer statue, the Washington Monument, the Sistine Chapel . . . well, everything, really. But the dog survives.

Terminator Salvation: "The End Begins. We Fight Back."
(Warner Bros./Photofest)

Afterword

RISE OF THE MACHINES

The War Against the Machines is over, and we never stood a chance. Try to make your way down any crowded sidewalk without continuously dodging humans hypnotized by the glowing screens of their latest iGadgets and you'll realize it's true. When *The Terminator* premiered in theaters in the fall of 1984, less than 8 percent of American households owned personal computers. Now we're outnumbered. According to a 2011 study by industry trade group CTIA–The Wireless Association, "there are 327.6 million active phones, computer tablets and laptops on cellular networks" in the United States, population 315.5 million. When Apple introduced its "Siri" personal assistant application for the iPhone, with its ability to answer spoken questions through a natural language interface, social networks like Twitter lit up with jokes about Skynet becoming self-aware.

We probably don't have to worry about our electronic devices turning on us just yet, but there's been a more insidious rise of the machines over the past couple of decades, and *Terminator* does bear some of the blame—or, more specifically, *Terminator 2*, with its quantum leap in the use of computer-generated imagery. In retrospect, it's as if James Cameron opened Pandora's box (no pun intended, *Avatar* fans). The use of CGI took another leap forward two years later, when Steven Spielberg employed the groundbreaking technology to bring dinosaurs back to life in *Jurassic Park*. For a while there, a palpable buzz of excitement surrounded digital effects; finally, our most talented filmmakers would be able to bring their most creative, mind-blowing visions to the screen. Nothing was impossible.

It hasn't exactly worked out that way. When it comes to the decline of movies as an art form, it's always fun to blame George Lucas, who has often been derided for his role in kick-starting Hollywood's blockbuster mentality with *Star Wars* in 1977. But that was a misdemeanor compared to the crimes against cinema he would perpetrate more than two decades later, when his prequel trilogy finally saw the light of day. At least the initial *Star Wars* trilogy is universally beloved (wildly out of proportion to its merits, yes, but universally beloved nonetheless); with their indigestible mix of tedious exposition, infantile cartoon characters, tin-eared dialogue, and wooden performances from the ostensibly real people in the cast, the prequels are grudgingly tolerated at best. Lucas stood revealed as a toymaker and merchandising mogul who had long since lost the human touch, and there's not enough industrial light and magic in the universe to make up for that.

Still, tempting as it may be to hold Lucas responsible for the current sorry state of special-effects-driven blockbusters, he had a lot of help along the way. Michael Bay certainly deserves singling out as one who has devalued the term *filmmaker* beyond recognition with his chaotic, CGI-saturated brand of action cinema. Bay's *Transformers* movies may have supplanted *Terminator* as America's favorite killer-robot franchise, but with their incoherent plotting, indifferent writing and acting, speed-freak editing, and inability to distinguish between bigger-and-better and louder-and-dumber, they're unlikely candidates to stand the test of time. Yet it's hard to hold even the most pandering filmmakers responsible when studio executives have grown increasingly reluctant to green-light any film that isn't based on an existing property. Of the top ten grossing movies of 2011, eight were sequels, while the remaining two were based on comic-book superheroes. Of course, that means you and I are at fault as well, every time we purchase a ticket to a movie we know is going to let us down, just because we want to turn off our brains for a couple of hours. (And when we pay twice as much for a would-be block-buster given a quickie 3D or IMAX conversion, well, who can say we don't deserve what we get?)

But why blame ourselves when we can blame Harry Knowles instead? The rise of geek culture was a byproduct of the Internet revolution we should have seen coming, and it was fun for a while, in a *Revenge of the Nerds* sort of way. Knowles launched his Ain't It Cool News site in 1996 as a way of keeping fans abreast of news and rumors about upcoming genre films. The writing on the site wasn't particularly strong, but the enthusiasm was contagious, as geeks finally had a venue to congregate and be heard outside of the comic-book shops. Somewhere along the way, however, outsiders became insiders, and the bullied became the bullies. Geekdom is now a cultural monolith; comic-book movies are our mainstream entertainments, and San Diego's annual Comic Con has transitioned from a gathering of fringe enthusiasts to the launching pad for the biggest Hollywood blockbusters. Numerous sites are dedicated to providing hourly updates on every phase of development and production for seemingly every genre film in the pipeline, but what's been lost along the way is the sense of discovery that came with opening day at the movie theater. Film criticism is all but dead as a profession, while indiscriminate bloggers for fan sites provide the studios with all the breathless blurbs they need to promote their product.

Yet while the future of science-fiction film generally looks bleak, there are always specific cases to remind us that the medium can still be put to creative, rewarding use. Some of the most intriguing sci-fi movies of recent vintage have been made independently, on small budgets; Duncan Jones' *Moon* and *Source Code*, 2011 Sundance favorite *Another Earth*, and British import *Attack the Block* have all found enthusiastic audiences, even if they haven't necessarily achieved box-office glory. One of the surprise hits of 2009 was Neill Blomkamp's *District 9*, a South African sci-fi film about an alien shantytown that demonstrated CGI could be used effectively and creatively for a moderate price tag. On a larger scale, Christopher Nolan's *Dark Knight* trilogy and unlikely brain-tickling blockbuster *Inception* have shown that mammoth entertainments don't have to be vacuous exercises in appealing to the lowest common denominator. The wonderful performance by Andy Serkis as the chimp Caesar in *Rise of the Planet of the Apes* would not have been possible without the recent advances in CGI and motion-capture technology. As long as talented, imaginative people can find a way to work within an extremely flawed system, there's always hope for the future of science fiction on the screen.

And what is the future of the Terminator? Predictably, the rights have changed hands yet again following *Terminator Salvation*. The Halcyon Company filed for Chapter 11 in 2009 and put the Terminator back on the auction block. The auction was won by Pacificor, the hedge fund that had financed Halcyon in the first place; Pacificor then turned around and launched its own bidding war for the rights to make *Terminator 5*. The winner was Oracle heiress Megan Ellison (no relation to Harlan), executive producer of the Coen Brothers' *True Grit* remake.

If *Terminator 5* gets made, it won't be with James Cameron at the helm; he's committed to two *Avatar* sequels due in 2014 and 2015. Action director Justin Lin was attached to the project but, due to scheduling conflicts with the sixth *Fast and the Furious* movie, may not be available either. But having completed his service to the people of California, Arnold Schwarzenegger has returned to acting and has let it be known he's ready to terminate again. Can *Terminator 5* somehow justify the existence of an elderly Terminator? Is there anything more to add to the saga, now that Judgment Day has come and gone? The future is not set, and there is no fate but what we make.

APPENDIX: ESSENTIAL DATA: 100 GREAT MOMENTS FROM SCIENCE-FICTION HISTORY

1. *Frankenstein* by Mary Shelley (1818, Lackington, Hughes, et al.)
2. *A Journey to the Center of the Earth* by Jules Verne (1864, Pierre-Jules Hetzel)
3. *The Time Machine* by H. G. Wells (1895, William Heinemann)
4. *A Trip to the Moon* (1902, Star Films, Georges Méliès, director)
5. *A Princess of Mars* by Edgar Rice Burroughs (1917, A. C. McClurg)
6. *Amazing Stories* (1926–2005, Hugo Gernsback, founder)
7. *Metropolis* (1927, UFA, Fritz Lang, director)
8. *Brave New World* by Aldous Huxley (1932, Chatto and Windus)
9. *Nineteen Eighty-Four* by George Orwell (1949, Secker and Warburg)
10. *The Martian Chronicles* by Ray Bradbury (1950, Doubleday)
11. *Weird Science* (1950–53, EC Comics, William Gaines and Al Feldstein, creators)
12. *The Thing from Another World* (1951, RKO, Christian Nyby and Howard Hawks [uncredited], directors)
13. *The Day the Earth Stood Still* (1951, 20th Century Fox, Robert Wise, director)
14. *Foundation* trilogy by Isaac Asimov (1951–53, Gnome Press)
15. *The Demolished Man* by Alfred Bester (1953, Galaxy Science Fiction)

16. *The War of the Worlds* (1953, Paramount, Byron Haskin, director)
17. *It Came from Outer Space* (1953, Universal, Jack Arnold, director)
18. *Invaders from Mars* (1953, 20th Century Fox, William Cameron Menzies, director)
19. *Childhood's End* by Arthur C. Clarke (1953, Ballantine)
20. *Fahrenheit 451* by Ray Bradbury (1953, Ballantine)
21. *Godzilla* (1954, Toho, Ishiro Honda, director)
22. *Invasion of the Body Snatchers* (1956, Allied Artists, Don Siegel, director)
23. *Forbidden Planet* (1956, MGM, Fred M. Wilcox, director)
24. *The Twilight Zone* (1959–64, CBS, Rod Serling, creator)
25. *The Time Machine* (1960, MGM, George Pal, director)
26. *Stranger in a Strange Land* by Robert A. Heinlein (1961, Putnam)
27. *A Canticle for Leibowitz* by Walter M. Miller Jr. (1961, J. P. Lippincott)
28. *The Man in the High Castle* by Philip K. Dick (1962, Putnam)
29. *La Jetée* (1962, Argos Films, Chris Marker, director)
30. *Doctor Who* (1963–present, BBC, Sydney Newman et al.)
31. *The Outer Limits* (1963–65, ABC, Leslie Stevens, creator)
32. *Dune* by Frank Herbert (1965, Chilton Books)
33. *Alphaville* (1965, Athos Films, Jean-Luc Godard, director)
34. *Star Trek* (1966–69, NBC, Gene Roddenberry, creator)
35. *The Prisoner* (1967–68, ITV, Patrick McGoohan, creator)
36. *Quatermass and the Pit* (1967, 20th Century Fox, Roy Ward Baker, director)
37. *2001: A Space Odyssey* (1968, MGM, Stanley Kubrick, director)
38. *Planet of the Apes* (1968, 20th Century Fox, Franklin J. Schaffner, director)
39. *Slaughterhouse-Five* by Kurt Vonnegut Jr. (1969, Delacorte)
40. *Ringworld* by Larry Niven (1970, Ballantine)
41. *Colossus: The Forbin Project* (1970, Universal, Joseph Sargent, director)
42. *THX 1138* (1971, Warner Bros., George Lucas, director)

43. *Riverworld* series by Philip José Farmer (1971–83, Putnam)
44. *A Clockwork Orange* (1971, Warner Bros., Stanley Kubrick, director)
45. *Solaris* (1972, Mosfilm, Andrei Tarkovsky, director)
46. *Silent Running* (1972, Universal, Douglas Trumbull, director)
47. *Conquest of the Planet of the Apes* (1972, 20th Century Fox, J. Lee Thompson, director)
48. *Sleeper* (1973, United Artists, Woody Allen, director)
49. *Fantastic Planet* (1973, Argos Films, René Laloux, director)
50. *The Dispossessed* by Ursula K. Le Guin (1974, Harper and Row)
51. *Deathbird Stories* by Harlan Ellison (1975, Harper and Row)
52. *The Man Who Fell to Earth* (1976, Columbia Pictures, Nicolas Roeg, director)
53. *Star Wars* (1977, 20th Century Fox, George Lucas, director)
54. *The Stand* by Stephen King (1978, Doubleday)
55. *Invasion of the Body Snatchers* (1978, United Artists, Philip Kaufman, director)
56. *Close Encounters of the Third Kind* (1978, Columbia, Steven Spielberg, director)
57. *The Hitchhiker's Guide to the Galaxy* (1978, BBC Radio 4, Douglas Adams, creator)
58. *Space Invaders* (1978, Taito, Tomohiro Nishikado, designer)
59. *Alien* (1979, 20th Century Fox, Ridley Scott, director)
60. *The Empire Strikes Back* (1980, 20th Century Fox, Irvin Kershner, director)
61. *Altered States* (1980, Warner Bros., Ken Russell, director)
62. *The Road Warrior* (aka *Mad Max 2*) (1981, Warner Bros., George Miller, director)
63. *Blade Runner* (1982, Warner Bros., Ridley Scott, director)
64. *E.T. the Extra-Terrestrial* (1982, Universal, Steven Spielberg, director)
65. *Star Trek II: The Wrath of Khan* (1982, Paramount, Nicholas Meyer, director)
66. *The Thing* (1982, Universal, John Carpenter, director)
67. *Neuromancer* by William Gibson (1984, Ace)

68. *Repo Man* (1984, Universal, Alex Cox, director)
69. *The Terminator* (1984, Orion, James Cameron, director)
70. *Back to the Future* (1985, Universal, Robert Zemeckis, director)
71. *Brazil* (1985, Universal, Terry Gilliam, director)
72. *The Handmaid's Tale* by Margaret Atwood (1985, McClelland and Stewart)
73. *Ender's Game* by Orson Scott Card (1986, Tor)
74. *The Fly* (1986, 20th Century Fox, David Cronenberg, director)
75. *Aliens* (1986, 20th Century Fox, James Cameron, director)
76. *Watchmen* by Alan Moore and Dave Gibbons (1986–87, DC Comics)
77. *Robocop* (1987, Orion, Paul Verhoeven, director)
78. *They Live* (1988, Universal, John Carpenter, director)
79. *Akira* (1988, Toho, Katsuhiro Otomo, director)
80. *Terminator 2: Judgment Day* (1991, TriStar, James Cameron, director)
81. *The X-Files* (1993–2002, Fox, Chris Carter, creator)
82. *12 Monkeys* (1995, Universal, Terry Gilliam, director)
83. *Ghost in the Shell* (1995, Shochiku, Mamoru Oshii, director)
84. *Starship Troopers* (1997, TriStar, Paul Verhoeven, director)
85. *Dark City* (1998, New Line, Alex Proyas, director)
86. *The Matrix* (1999, Warner Bros., Larry and Andy Wachowski, directors)
87. *Cryptonomicon* by Neal Stephenson (1999, Avon)
88. *Donnie Darko* (2001, Newmarket, Richard Kelly, director)
89. *Y: The Last Man* by Brian K. Vaughan and Pia Guerra (2002–8, Vertigo)
90. *Eternal Sunshine of the Spotless Mind* (2004, Focus, Michel Gondry, director)
91. *Primer* (2004, ThinkFilm, Shane Carruth, director)
92. *Lost* (2004–2010, ABC, Damon Lindelof et al., creators)
93. *Battlestar Galactica* (2004–9, SciFi, Ronald D. Moore et al., creators)
94. *The Road* by Cormac McCarthy (2006, Alfred A. Knopf)

95. *A Scanner Darkly* (2006, Warner Independent, Richard Linklater, director)
96. *Bioshock* (2007, 2K Boston, Ken Levine, designer)
97. *WALL-E* (2008, Pixar, Andrew Stanton, director)
98. *Fringe* (2008–present, Fox, Robert Orci et al., creators)
99. *Inception* (2010, Warner Bros., Christopher Nolan, director)
100. *Portal 2* (2011, Valve, Joshua Weier, designer)

BIBLIOGRAPHY

Agel, Jerome, ed., *The Making of Kubrick's 2001* (Signet, 1970).

Anderson, Craig W., *Science Fiction Films of the Seventies* (McFarland, 1985).

Andrews, Nigel, *True Myths: The Life and Times of Arnold Schwarzenegger* (Birch Lane Press, 1996).

Benson, Michael, *Vintage Science Fiction Films, 1896–1949* (McFarland, 1985).

Booker, M. Keith, *Science Fiction Television* (Praeger, 2004).

Brown, Richard, and Kevin S. Decker, eds., *Terminator and Philosophy: I'll Be Back, Therefore I Am* (John Wiley and Sons, 2009).

Ciment, Michel, *Kubrick: The Definitive Edition* (Faber and Faber, 2003).

Ellison, Harlan, *Harlan Ellison's The City on the Edge of Forever: The Original Teleplay That Became the Classic Star Trek Episode* (White Wolf, 1996).

Ellison, Harlan, *Harlan Ellison's Watching* (Underwood-Miller, 1989).

Fleming, Michael, "Arnold Back for 'Westworld,' 'Conan' Redos," *Variety*, March 13, 2002.

Flynn, John L., *The Films of Arnold Schwarzenegger* (Citadel Press, 1993).

French, Sean, *The Terminator* (BFI Modern Classics, 1996).

Goldberg, Lee, et al., *Science Fiction Filmmaking in the 1980s* (McFarland, 1995).

Goodyear, Dana, "Man of Extremes: The Return of James Cameron," *The New Yorker*, October 26, 2009.

Greene, Eric, *Planet of the Apes as American Myth: Race, Politics, and Popular Culture* (Wesleyan, 1998).

Griggs, Brandon, "Inventor Unveils $7,000 Talking Sex Robot," CNN, February 1, 2010.

Hamsher, Jane, *Killer Instinct* (Broadway, 1997).

Hefley, Robert M., and Howard Zimmerman, *Robots* (Starlog Press, 1980).

Hofstede, David, *Planet of the Apes: An Unofficial Companion* (ECW Press, 2001).

IGN.com, "Guiding the Sarah Connor Chronicles," June 20, 2007.

Jermyn, Deborah, and Sean Redmond, eds., *The Cinema of Kathryn Bigelow: Hollywood Transgressor* (Wallflower Press, 2003).

Keegan, Rebecca, *The Futurist: The Life and Films of James Cameron* (Crown Archetype, 2009).

Meehan, Paul, *Tech-Noir: The Fusion of Science Fiction and Film Noir* (McFarland, 2008).

Minden, Michael, and Holger Bachmann, eds., *Fritz Lang's Metropolis: Cinematic Visions of Technology and Fear* (Camden House, 2000).

Mitchell, Charles P., *A Guide to Apocalyptic Cinema* (Greenwood Press, 2001).

Parisi, Paula, *Titanic and the Making of James Cameron: The Inside Story of the Three-Year Adventure That Rewrote Motion Picture History* (Newmarket Press, 1998).

Phillips, Mark, and Frank Garcia, *Science Fiction Television Series: Episode Guides, Histories and Casts and Credits for 62 Prime Time Shows, 1959 Through 1989* (McFarland, 1996).

Redmond, Sean, ed., *Liquid Metal: The Science Fiction Film Reader* (Wallflower Press, 2004).

Robb, Brian J., *Counterfeit Worlds: Philip K. Dick on Film* (Titan Books, 2006).

Russo, Joe, et al., *Planet of the Apes Revisited: The Behind-the-Scenes Story of the Classic Science Fiction Saga* (St. Martin's Griffin, 2001).

Scalzi, John, *The Rough Guide to Sci-Fi Movies* (Rough Guide Ltd., 2005).
Schow, David J., and Jeffrey Frentzen, *The Outer Limits: The Official Companion* (Ace Science Fiction Books, 1986).
Shapiro, Marc, *James Cameron: An Unauthorized Biography of the Filmmaker* (Renaissance Books, 2000).
Shay, Don, and Jody Duncan, *The Making of Terminator 2: Judgment Day* (Bantam Books, 1991).
Saunders, Dave, *Arnold: Schwarzenegger and the Movies* (I. B. Tauris, 2009).
Warren, Bill, *Keep Watching the Skies!: American Science Fiction Movies of the Fifties, The 21st Century Edition* (McFarland, 2010).
Williams, Tony, ed., *George A. Romero: Interviews* (University Press of Mississippi, 2011).

INDEX

INDEX